Computers

For

Beginners and Seniors

The Most User-Friendly Step By Step Guide For Seniors and Beginners to Master Their Computer with Ease and Confidence

Dale Pearce

Copyright © 2023 by Dale Pearce

No part of this publication may be reproduced, stored in a retrieval system, or transmitted in any form or by any means, electronic, mechanical, photocopying, recording, scanning, or otherwise, without the express written permission of the Publisher

INTRODUCTION 8

WHY THIS BOOK? 8
HOW TO USE THIS BOOK 9
UNDERSTANDING TECHNOLOGY JARGON 11

CHAPTER 1: GETTING ACQUAINTED WITH COMPUTERS 15

WHAT IS A COMPUTER? 15
TYPES OF COMPUTERS 16

COMPONENTS OF A COMPUTER SYSTEM 18

UNDERSTANDING COMPUTER HARDWARE 19

NAVIGATING THE OPERATING SYSTEM 23

INTRODUCTION TO OPERATING SYSTEMS 23
WINDOWS 24
MACOS 25
LINUX 27
WINDOWS COMPUTER TO BUY 28
HOW TO SETUP YOUR COMPUTER 30
Step 1: Unboxing and Inspection *30*
Step 2: Finding a Suitable Location *30*
Step 3: Connecting Hardware *30*
Step 4: Turning On the Computer *31*
Step 5: Setting Up Windows *31*
Step 6: Installing Software and Applications *31*
Step 7: Personalizing Your Desktop *32*
Step 8: Configuring Additional Peripherals *32*
Step 9: Creating Backups *32*

CHAPTER 2 35

LEARNING THE BASICS 35
Knowing and Mastering Your Compter Keyboard *35*
Connecting your Computer to the Internet *38*
The Desktop of Your Computer System *40*
CHAPTER 3 44
WORKING WITH APPLICATIONS 44
Installing New Applications: *44*
Accessing Installed Applications *45*

CHAPTER 4 46

STAYING SAFE ONLINE 46

UNDERSTANDING INTERNET SECURITY 46
Malware *46*
Phishing *46*
Cyberattacks *46*
ANTIVIRUS AND ANTI-MALWARE SOFTWARE 46
PASSWORD MANAGEMENT: 47
TWO-FACTOR AUTHENTICATION (2FA): 47

Network Security	47
Data Backups	48

CHAPTER 5 49

BASIC TROUBLESHOOTING 49

Windows	49
macOS:	50

CHAPTER 6 52

INTRODUCTION TO SOCIAL MEDIA 52

FACEBOOK: 52

2. X (TWITTER): 53

3. LINKEDIN: 54

4. INSTAGRAM: 54

PRIVACY SETTINGS 56

1. FACEBOOK: 56

Profile Privacy:	56
Timeline and Tagging:	56
Apps and Websites:	56

2. X(TWITTER): 56

Adjusting Privacy Settings:	56
Tweet Privacy:	56
Account Privacy:	57

3. LINKEDIN: 57

Adjusting Privacy Settings:	57
Profile Privacy:	57
Activity Broadcasts:	57

4. INSTAGRAM: 57

Adjusting Privacy Settings:	57
Account Privacy:	57
Activity Status:	57
Story Controls:	57
Connecting with Friends and Family	58

CHAPTER 7 61

EXPLORING MULTIMEDIA 61

Photos and Images	63
Music & Videos	66
Managing and Enjoying Multimedia Content	69
Organizing Photo Albums	72
Playing Music and Videos	75

CHAPTER 8 78

MICROSOFT WORD 78
GETTING STARTED WITH MICROSOFT WORD 78
INSTALLING MICROSOFT WORD 87

EXPLORING THE WORD INTERFACE 90
RIBBON 90
HOME TAB 92
INSERT TAB 93
LAYOUT TAB 94

BACKSTAGE VIEW 96
ACCESSING BACKSTAGE VIEW FOR DOCUMENT MANAGEMENT 96
FILE OPTIONS, SAVING, AND OPENING DOCUMENTS. 98

QUICK ACCESS TOOLBAR 100
CUSTOMIZING THE QUICK ACCESS TOOLBAR 100
ADDING COMMANDS TO THE QUICK ACCESS TOOLBAR 102
REMOVING COMMANDS FROM THE QUICK ACCESS TOOLBAR 103

NAVIGATING A DOCUMENT 104
USING THE MOUSE: 104
USING THE KEYBOARD: 104
USING THE NAVIGATION PANE: 105
USING GO TO: 105
SCROLL BARS: 106
PAGE NAVIGATION: 106
KEYBOARD SHORTCUTS: 107

DOCUMENT FORMATTING 109
FONT STYLES AND SIZES 109
Changing Fonts: *109*
Applying Font Styles: *109*
Changing Font Size: *109*
Combining Font Formatting: *110*
Quick Font Formatting Tips: *110*
USING THE RIBBON: 111
Bold: *111*
Italic: *111*
Underline: *111*
Clearing Formatting: *112*

PARAGRAPH ALIGNMENT AND LINE SPACING 113
LEFT ALIGN: 113
CENTER ALIGN: 113
RIGHT ALIGN: 113
JUSTIFY: 114
ADJUSTING LINE SPACING FOR READABILITY 115

LISTS AND BULLETS 117

- Creating Bulleted And Numbered Lists 117
- Customizing List Styles. 119

PAGE SETUP AND MARGINS 121

TYPING AND EDITING TEXT 125

COPYING, CUTTING, AND PASTING 130

FIND AND REPLACE 135

SPELL CHECK AND GRAMMAR 137

CHAPTER 9 142

MICROSOFT EXCEL 142
- Getting Started with Excel 142

INSTALLATION AND SETUP 145
- Configuring Excel Preferences 147

THE EXCEL INTERFACE 150
- Ribbon and Tabs 150
- Cells, Rows, and Columns 152

ENTERING AND FORMATTING DATA 156

FORMULAS AND FUNCTIONS 162
- Formula Structure: 162
- Operators: 162
- Cell References: 162
- SUM Function: 162
- AVERAGE Function: 162
- IF Function: 163
- VLOOKUP Function: 163
- COUNT Function: 163
- CONCATENATE Function: 163
- NOW Function: 163

FORMULA AUDITING TOOLS: 163

ERROR CHECKING: 164

FORMULA TIPS: 164

PERFORMING BASIC ARITHMETIC OPERATIONS 165
- Addition: 165
- Subtraction: 165
- Multiplication: 165
- Division: 165
- Using Cell References: 166
- Using Parentheses: 166
- AutoSum Feature: 166
- Absolute and Relative References: 166
- Error Handling: 167

DATA VISUALIZATION WITH CHARTS 168

    CREATING CHARTS IN EXCEL 168
    FORMATTING AND CUSTOMIZING CHARTS 172

SORTING AND FILTERING DATA 175

    SORTING DATA IN EXCEL 175
        Sorting a Range of Data: 175
        Sorting by Custom Order: 176
        Sorting an Excel Table: 176
        Sorting with Keyboard Shortcuts: 176
        Sorting Multiple Columns: 176
        Undoing a Sort: 177
    FILTERING DATA 177
        Basic Filtering: 177
        Applying Filters: 177
        Multiple Criteria Filtering: 178
        Clearing Filters: 178
        Advanced Filter Options: 178
        Multiple Criteria Filtering: 178
        Filtered Data Analysis: 179

DATA PROTECTION AND SECURITY 180

    PROTECTING WORKSHEETS AND WORKBOOKS 180
    USING PASSWORDS AND PERMISSIONS 180

INTRODUCTION TO PIVOTTABLES 183

    CREATING PIVOTTABLES 183
        Basic PivotTable Creation: 183
        PivotTable Field List: 183
        Customizing PivotTable: 184
        Creating PivotCharts: 184
        Advanced PivotTable Options: 184

DATA IMPORT AND EXPORT 186

    IMPORTING DATA INTO EXCEL 186
        Importing Data from a Text File (CSV): 186
        Importing Data from Other Sources: 186
        Importing Data from Excel Files: 187
        Refreshing Imported Data: 187
    EXPORTING DATA FROM EXCEL 188
        Save As a Different File Format: 188
        Save a Specific Range as a CSV: 189
        Exporting a Chart or Graph: 189
        Save a Worksheet as a PDF: 190

EXCEL TIPS AND TRICKS FOR SENIORS & BEGINNERS 191

COMMON ERRORS AND TROUBLESHOOTING 197

    IDENTIFYING AND FIXING ERRORS 197

- *Common Types of Errors:* 197
- *Identifying Errors:* 197
- *Resolving Errors:* 197
- *Excel Tools for Error Resolution:* 198

TROUBLESHOOTING COMMON EXCEL ISSUES 199
1. EXCEL CRASHES OR FREEZES: 199
2. EXCEL FORMULAS NOT UPDATING: 199
3. DATA NOT SORTING CORRECTLY: 199
4. EXCEL FILE WON'T OPEN: 199
5. EXCEL FILE IS TOO LARGE: 200
6. PRINT PREVIEW DOESN'T MATCH ACTUAL PRINT: 200
7. CANNOT COPY-PASTE DATA: 200
8. CELL FORMATTING ISSUES: 200
9. GRAPHS/CHARTS NOT DISPLAYING PROPERLY: 201
10. ERROR MESSAGES IN FORMULAS: 201
11. MISSING DATA AFTER FILTERING: 201

CONCLUSION 202

Introduction
Why This Book?

Welcome to Computers for Beginners and seniors. In this introductory section, we aim to provide you with a clear understanding of the purpose and value of this book, helping you embark on your journey to computer literacy with confidence.

Computers have woven themselves into the fabric of modern life, offering boundless opportunities for communication, learning, entertainment, and productivity. However, we understand that diving into the world of technology can be both exciting and daunting, especially for beginners and seniors who might be encountering computers for the first time or seeking to enhance their existing knowledge.

This book was meticulously crafted to bridge the gap between the unfamiliar and the accessible. Our goal is to empower you, whether you're a tech newcomer or someone who wants to catch up with the rapidly evolving digital landscape. **Here's why this book is your ideal companion:**

1. Tailored for All Skill Levels: We recognize that everyone starts somewhere. Whether you've never touched a keyboard before or you've dabbled but want to delve deeper, this book covers a range of topics at a comfortable pace. Our approach combines simplicity with depth, allowing beginners to grasp fundamentals and providing seniors with tools to enhance their computer experience.

2. Practical and Hands-On: Theory is important, but practical skills are what truly empower you. Each chapter is designed with hands-on activities and step-by-step guides to ensure that you not only understand the concepts but can apply them to real-world situations. From setting up an email account to customizing your desktop, you'll gain confidence through practice.

3. Friendly Language: We believe that technical jargon should never stand in the way of learning. Our friendly and approachable language ensures that complex concepts are explained in a manner that's easy to understand. We've made it a priority to create an environment where you feel comfortable asking questions and exploring without hesitation.

4. Focus on Seniors: Recognizing the unique needs and concerns of seniors, this book dedicates special attention to addressing these considerations. From larger font sizes to tips for navigating accessibility features, we want to make your computer journey as enjoyable as possible.

5. Comprehensive Coverage: Computers are multifaceted tools, and we've left no stone unturned. From understanding the basics of hardware and software to navigating the internet, communicating online, creating documents, and ensuring your computer's security, each aspect is explored thoroughly.

6. Adaptable Pace: Learning is a journey, not a sprint. Feel free to proceed at your own pace, revisiting chapters as needed. The book is structured to accommodate different learning styles and preferences, ensuring that you're in control of your learning experience.

7. Empowerment and Independence: Our ultimate aim is to arm you with the skills you need to navigate the digital realm with confidence and independence. By the time you've journeyed through these pages, you'll possess a solid foundation for using computers for personal, social, and practical purposes.

In a world where technology evolves rapidly, understanding computers is no longer a luxury – it's a necessity. This book is your steppingstone into this exciting realm. So, whether you're a beginner ready to take your first keystrokes or a senior looking to embark on a new digital adventure, rest assured that "Computers for Beginners and Seniors" has been thoughtfully created to guide you every step of the way. Welcome aboard!

How to Use This Book

Welcome to "Computers for Beginners and Seniors"! We're thrilled that you've chosen to join us on this journey of discovery and learning. To make the most of your experience with this book, let's walk through how to navigate and utilize its contents effectively.

1. Start with the Introduction:

Begin by reading the introduction. It provides an overview of what to expect from the book and why it's a valuable resource for you. Understanding the purpose and structure of the book will help you approach the content with enthusiasm and confidence.

2. Follow the Sequence:

The chapters are organized in a logical sequence, gradually building your knowledge and skills. It's recommended to start from Chapter 1 and progress sequentially. Each chapter builds upon the previous one, ensuring a smooth learning curve.

3. Take It Step by Step:

Within each chapter, you'll find concepts broken down into manageable steps. We understand that technology might feel overwhelming at times, but don't worry – we're here to guide you every step of the way. Read through the explanations, follow the instructions, and practice the exercises provided.

4. Engage with Exercises and Examples:

Throughout the book, you'll encounter exercises and examples that reinforce the concepts you're learning. These practical activities are designed to help you apply your newfound knowledge, making the learning process more interactive and memorable.

5. Pause and Reflect:

Feel free to pause and reflect after completing a chapter or section. Take a moment to absorb the information and ensure you're comfortable with the material before moving on. Don't hesitate to revisit earlier sections if needed; repetition is a great way to solidify your understanding.

6. Notes and Highlights:

Consider keeping a notebook handy as you read. Jot down key points, new terms you've learned, or any questions that come to mind. You can also highlight sections in the book itself to easily refer back to important information.

7. Practical Application:

The real magic happens when you apply what you've learned. As you progress, try using your computer to practice the skills discussed in the book. Experiment, explore, and don't be afraid to make mistakes – they're a natural part of learning.

8. Review and Recap:

At the end of each chapter, there may be a summary or key takeaways. Reviewing these summaries can help reinforce what you've learned and serve as a quick reference in the future.

9. Go at Your Own Pace:

Remember, there's no rush. Learning is a journey, and everyone progresses at their own pace. If a particular topic seems challenging, take the time to revisit it and practice until you're comfortable.

10. Enjoy the Experience:

Learning about computers can be a fun and rewarding experience. Embrace the journey, celebrate your achievements, and don't forget to enjoy the new possibilities that technology brings to your fingertips.

Understanding Technology Jargon

As you embark on your quest to become tech-savvy, it's important to familiarize yourself with some common technology jargon. While these terms may seem intimidating at first, they are like the keys to a secret language that unlocks the potential of the digital world. Let's dive in and demystify some of these terms.

1. Hardware and Software:

Hardware: These are the physical components of a computer or device, like the monitor, keyboard, and hard drive. Think of it as the tangible parts you can touch.

Software: Software refers to the programs, applications, and operating systems that run on the hardware. It's the invisible force that makes your computer perform specific tasks.

2. Operating System:

The operating system (OS) is the software that manages and controls the computer's hardware and software. It provides the user interface and allows you to interact with the computer.

3. Browser:

A browser is a software application used to access and view websites on the internet. Common browsers include Chrome, Firefox, and Safari.

4. URL:

URL stands for Uniform Resource Locator. It's the web address that you type into a browser's address bar to access a specific website. For example, "www.example.com" is a URL.

5. Wi-Fi:

Wi-Fi is a wireless technology that allows devices to connect to the internet without using physical cables. It enables you to access the internet from various locations within range of a wireless router.

6. RAM (Random Access Memory):
RAM is the computer's short-term memory. It stores data that is actively being used by the computer's software. More RAM generally means smoother and faster performance.

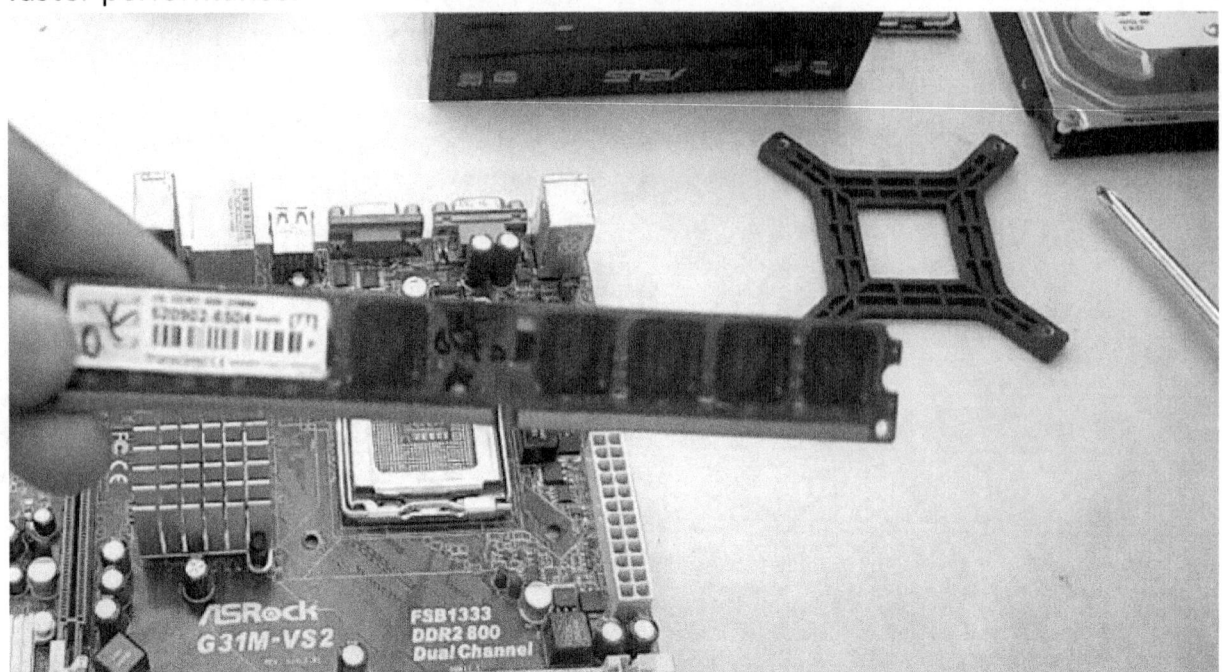

7. Hard Drive (HDD) and Solid State Drive (SSD):
These are storage devices for your computer. HDDs use spinning disks to store data, while SSDs use flash memory. SSDs are generally faster and more reliable.

8. Cloud Computing:
Cloud computing involves storing and accessing data and programs over the internet rather than on a local computer. It allows you to access your files and applications from anywhere with an internet connection.

9. Firewall:
A firewall is a security system that acts as a barrier between your computer and potential threats from the internet. It monitors and controls incoming and outgoing network traffic.

10. Malware:
Malware is short for malicious software. It includes viruses, spyware, and other harmful programs designed to damage or steal information from your computer.

11. Browser Cookies:
Cookies are small pieces of data stored by websites on your computer. They can remember your preferences and login information, making your browsing experience more convenient.

12. IP Address:
An IP address is a unique numerical label assigned to each device connected to a computer network. It's like the "address" that allows devices to communicate with each other over the internet.

This technology jargon might seem overwhelming at first, but as you continue to explore and learn, these terms will become second nature. You can always refer back to this guide whenever you encounter a new term.

Chapter 1: Getting Acquainted with Computers

What is a Computer?

A computer is a remarkable device that performs tasks, processes information, and enables communication in ways that were once beyond imagination. It's like a versatile tool that can transform ideas into reality, connecting people and ideas across the globe.

1. The Basics:

At its core, a computer is made up of hardware and software. Imagine it as a combination of a physical body and a mind.

2. Hardware - The Physical Parts:

The hardware of a computer consists of tangible, physical components that you can see and touch. These include:

Central Processing Unit (CPU): Often referred to as the brain of the computer, the CPU processes instructions and performs calculations.

Monitor: The screen where you can see what's happening on the computer. It's like the computer's window to the digital world.

Keyboard: A set of keys that you use to type and input information.

Mouse or Touchpad: An input device that allows you to interact with the computer by moving a cursor on the screen.

Memory (RAM): This is where the computer stores information it's currently using, like the desk space you use to work on tasks.

Storage (Hard Drive or SSD): Similar to a filing cabinet, storage holds all the files, documents, and programs that you use.

Ports: These are like the computer's connection points. They allow you to plug in external devices like USB drives, printers, and headphones.

3. Software - The Digital Mind:

Software is the intangible part of the computer that tells it what to do. Just like your thoughts guide your actions, software guides the computer's operations. There are two main types of software:

Operating System (OS): This is the software that manages the computer's hardware and allows you to interact with it. It's like the conductor of an orchestra, coordinating all the parts to play in harmony.

Applications (Apps): These are the programs you use to perform specific tasks. For example, word processors like Microsoft Word or web browsers like Google Chrome are applications.

4. How Computers Work:
Computers follow instructions in a sequence. Imagine it like following a recipe in a cookbook. These instructions are written in programming languages that the computer understands.

5. Connecting and Communicating:
Computers can be connected to each other through networks, like the internet. This enables people to share information, communicate, and collaborate regardless of their physical locations.

Types of Computers

1. Personal Computers (PCs):
These are the computers most of us are familiar with. Personal computers come in two main flavors:

Desktop Computers: These are stationary computers designed to sit on a desk. They consist of a separate monitor, CPU, keyboard, and mouse. Desktops are known for their power and versatility.

Laptop Computers: Laptops are portable versions of desktops. They combine the monitor, keyboard, touchpad, and CPU in a single device. Laptops offer the convenience of computing on the go.

2. Tablets:

Tablets are slim, lightweight devices with touchscreens. They're like a blend of a laptop and a smartphone. Tablets are great for browsing the internet, watching videos, reading books, and playing games.

3. Smartphones:
While you might primarily think of smartphones as communication devices, they are also incredibly capable computers. Smartphones are pocket-sized computers that allow you to make calls, send messages, browse the internet, use apps, and more.

4. Servers:
Servers are computers designed to provide services to other computers over a network. They handle tasks like storing files, hosting websites, managing email, and serving as the backbone of the internet.

5. Workstations:
Workstations are high-performance computers used for specialized tasks like graphic design, video editing, 3D modeling, and scientific research. They are designed to handle demanding applications with ease.

6. Mainframes:
Mainframe computers are powerful machines used by large organizations to manage vast amounts of data and perform complex calculations. They play a crucial role in industries like finance, healthcare, and telecommunications.

7. Supercomputers:
Supercomputers are the giants of computing. They're incredibly powerful and are used for tasks that require immense processing power, such as weather forecasting, scientific simulations, and complex data analysis.

8. Embedded Computers:

Embedded computers are tucked inside other devices and perform specific functions. You encounter them in everyday objects like cars, appliances, digital cameras, and even your microwave.

9. Wearable Computers:

Wearable computers are integrated into clothing or accessories. Smartwatches and fitness trackers are common examples. They help you track your health, receive notifications, and even make calls.

10. IoT Devices (Internet of Things):

IoT devices are everyday objects that are connected to the internet, allowing them to communicate and share data. Smart thermostats, smart home assistants, and even connected light bulbs fall into this category.

11. Gaming Consoles:

Gaming consoles are specialized computers designed for gaming. They offer immersive gaming experiences and can also be used for media playback and online services.

The world of computers is diverse and ever evolving. Each type of computer caters to specific needs and preferences. Whether you're looking for portability, power, or specialization, there's a type of computer tailored for you.

As you explore the possibilities of these different computer types, you're embarking on a journey that promises endless learning and discovery. Embrace the diversity of computers, and with each new understanding, you'll be better equipped to navigate the digital landscape with confidence and curiosity.

Components of a Computer System

Central Processing Unit (CPU)
Memory (RAM)
Storage (Hard Drive or SSD)
Motherboard

Power Supply Unit (PSU)
Graphics Processing Unit (GPU)
Input and Output Devices (Keyboard, Mouse, Monitor, Printer, etc.)
Expansion Cards (Sound Card, Wi-Fi Card, etc.)
Cooling System (Fans, Heat Sinks)
Case/Chassis
Optical Drive (CD/DVD/Blu-ray)
Ports and Connectors (USB, HDMI, Ethernet, etc.)
BIOS/UEFI
Network Interface Card (NIC)
Sound Card
Speakers or Headphones

Understanding Computer Hardware

Computer hardware refers to the physical components that make up your computer. Let's break down some key elements and explore how they work: Imagine a workshop filled with tools, each serving a unique purpose. Computer hardware is akin to these tools, coming together to create a powerful device that transforms your ideas into reality.

1. Central Processing Unit (CPU):

Imagine the CPU as the brain of the computer. It's responsible for executing instructions and performing calculations. When you open a program or perform any task on your computer, the CPU is at the heart of making it happen.

2. Memory (RAM):

RAM is like the computer's short-term memory. When you run a program, it's loaded into RAM so that the CPU can access it quickly. The more RAM you have, the more programs and data your computer can handle at once.

3. Storage (Hard Drive or SSD):

Consider storage as the computer's long-term memory. It's where all your files, documents, and programs are stored, even when the computer is turned off. Hard drives and solid-state drives (SSDs) are two common types of storage devices.

4. Motherboard:

The motherboard is like the backbone of the computer. It connects all the components, including the CPU, memory, and storage, allowing them to communicate and work together seamlessly.

5. Power Supply Unit (PSU):

The PSU is responsible for supplying power to all the components. It ensures that your computer has the necessary energy to function.

6. Graphics Processing Unit (GPU):

The GPU, also known as a graphics card, handles tasks related to displaying images and videos. It's especially important for tasks like gaming and video editing, where graphics performance is crucial.

7. Input and Output Devices:

Input devices like keyboards and mice allow you to provide commands to the computer. Output devices like monitors and printers display information and provide tangible results of your actions.

8. Expansion Cards:

These are optional components that can be added to the motherboard to enhance the computer's capabilities. For example, a sound card can improve audio quality, and a Wi-Fi card can enable wireless connectivity.

9. Cooling System:

Computers generate heat as they operate. The cooling system, which can include fans and heat sinks, helps keep the temperature within safe limits to prevent overheating.

How They Work Together:

Imagine a symphony orchestra. Each instrument has its role, but they harmonize to create beautiful music. Similarly, computer components work together in harmony:

You press a key on the keyboard (input).
The keyboard sends a signal to the CPU.
The CPU processes the signal and displays the corresponding letter on the screen (output).
The data is temporarily stored in RAM.
If you save the document, it's written to the storage device (hard drive or SSD) for long-term storage.

Interacting with Software:

When you open a program or app, the CPU fetches instructions from the storage and loads them into RAM. The CPU processes these instructions, interacting with other components like the GPU to display graphics and the storage to retrieve data.

In summary, a computer system is a symphony of components working together to process information, execute tasks, and deliver the results you see on the screen. Each part plays a vital role in creating the seamless digital experiences we enjoy every day.

By understanding how these components collaborate, you'll gain insight into the magic that powers your computer. As you continue your journey, you'll find that your knowledge empowers you to use technology more confidently and explore the endless possibilities of the digital realm.

Navigating the Operating System

Introduction to Operating Systems

In this guide, we'll embark on a journey to understand the pivotal role that operating systems play in the world of computers. Picture the operating system as the conductor of a grand symphony, harmonizing the various components of your computer to create a seamless and enjoyable experience.

1. Defining the Operating System: At its core, an operating system (OS) is a software that acts as the intermediary between you, the user, and the computer's hardware. Think of it as the bridge that enables you to communicate with your computer and make it perform tasks.

2. A Unified Control Center: Imagine the OS as the captain of a ship. It manages and coordinates every aspect of your computer, from starting up and shutting down to managing files, running applications, and connecting to the internet. Just as a conductor guides musicians to create beautiful music, the OS orchestrates the various components to create a harmonious digital experience.

3. User Interface: The user interface is like the language you use to communicate with your computer. It provides a visual way for you to interact with the computer, whether through clicking icons, typing commands, or using touch gestures.

4. Types of Operating Systems: There are several types of operating systems, each tailored to specific devices and needs:

Desktop Operating Systems: These are designed for personal computers and laptops. Examples include Windows, macOS, and Linux.

Mobile Operating Systems: These run on smartphones and tablets. You might be familiar with iOS (Apple devices) and Android (used by various manufacturers).

Server Operating Systems: These power servers that provide services over networks, such as hosting websites or managing email.

Embedded Operating Systems: These are found in devices like ATMs, digital cameras, and smart appliances.

5. Multitasking and Memory Management: Imagine you're juggling multiple tasks. The OS enables your computer to multitask as well. It allocates memory to different programs, making sure they don't interfere with each other. This allows you to run a web browser, listen to music, and edit a document simultaneously.

6. File Management: The OS helps you manage your digital files just like a librarian organizes books. It creates, stores, copies, and organizes files and folders, making it easy for you to find and access your information.

7. Software and Compatibility: When you install software (applications), the OS ensures they run smoothly. It manages resources, resolves conflicts, and keeps your system stable. It's like the referee that ensures everyone follows the rules of the game.

8. Updates and Security: The OS also ensures your computer stays secure and up to date. It provides regular updates to fix bugs, enhance features, and protect against security threats.

9. Booting Up: When you turn on your computer, the OS comes to life. It manages the startup process, initializes hardware, and loads essential components into memory, readying your computer for your commands.

Windows

Windows is an operating system developed by Microsoft. It's the software that runs on your computer, providing you with a visual interface to interact with your device and perform a wide array of tasks.

1. The Desktop and User Interface: When you first start your computer, you're greeted by the desktop, which is like your digital workspace. Icons represent files, folders, and applications, making it easy for you to access what you need. The Start Menu is your command center, offering a gateway to your apps, documents, and settings.

2. Applications and Software: Windows supports a variety of applications, or "apps," that enable you to perform tasks. Whether it's browsing the web, writing documents, managing photos, or sending emails, there's an app for nearly every need.

4. File Management with Windows Explorer: Imagine Windows Explorer as your digital filing cabinet. It helps you organize, copy, move, and search for files and folders. You can even create folders within folders, just like organizing papers in real life.

5. Customization and Personalization: Windows understands that your computer should reflect your style. You can personalize your desktop background, screen savers, and even colors to make your computer truly your own.

6. Taskbar and Notification Center: The taskbar is like your navigation hub. It contains the Start button, open applications, and a handy system tray. The notification center keeps you informed about updates, messages, and events.

7. Multitasking Made Easy: Windows excels at multitasking. You can have multiple applications open at once, easily switching between them. Imagine it like having multiple books open on your desk, each waiting for your attention.

8. Internet and Browsing: Windows includes the Microsoft Edge web browser, allowing you to explore the vast expanse of the internet. Just like a library, the internet is filled with information, entertainment, and ways to connect with others.

9. Updates and Security: Windows regularly updates to enhance features and security. Updates ensure that your computer is protected against threats and equipped with the latest tools.

MacOS

macOS is the operating system that powers Apple's Mac computers. Renowned for its elegance and user-friendly interface, macOS is designed to provide a smooth and engaging environment for both creative tasks and everyday computing.

2. User Interface - The macOS Experience: macOS boasts a distinctive user interface characterized by its clean design and ease of use. The Dock, located at the bottom of the screen, gives you quick access to your favorite apps. The Menu Bar at the top provides convenient access to system functions and settings.

3. **Spotlight Search:** Imagine having a digital assistant at your fingertips. Spotlight Search allows you to find files, launch apps, perform calculations, and even access information on the web—all by typing a few keywords.

4. Applications - The Apple Ecosystem: macOS comes with a suite of powerful applications that cater to various needs. Apps like Safari (web browser), Mail (email client), and Preview (PDF viewer) are seamlessly integrated to enhance your productivity and creativity.

5. Finder - Your Digital Workspace: Finder is the macOS file management tool that helps you organize, search, and access your files. It's like a digital version of a filing cabinet, enabling you to keep your documents in order.

6. iCloud Integration: With iCloud, Apple's cloud storage service, your files, photos, and documents can be accessed and synchronized across all your Apple devices. This integration ensures your data is always up to date and accessible.

7. Continuity - Seamlessly Connected Devices: Imagine starting an email on your Mac and finishing it on your iPhone. Continuity allows you to seamlessly switch between Apple devices, making multitasking and communication effortless.

8. Security and Privacy: macOS places a strong emphasis on security and privacy. Features like Gatekeeper help protect your system from malicious software, while the Privacy preferences allow you to control which apps have access to your data.

9. Updates and Upgrades: Apple regularly releases updates to enhance the functionality and security of macOS. These updates can be easily installed, ensuring your system remains optimized and protected.

10. Accessibility: macOS is designed to be inclusive. The Accessibility features empower users with diverse needs to customize their experience and use their Mac with ease.

Linux

Linux is an open-source operating system kernel that forms the foundation for a wide range of operating systems, known as "Linux distributions" or "distros." Linux distributions are developed by diverse communities, creating a rich ecosystem of options catering to different needs and preferences.

2. **Open-Source Philosophy:** Linux embodies the open-source philosophy, allowing users to access, modify, and distribute its source code. This promotes collaboration, transparency, and the collective improvement of the system.

3. **Variety of Distributions:** The beauty of Linux lies in its diversity. Various distributions cater to different use cases and audiences. Examples include Ubuntu, Fedora, Debian, and CentOS. Each distribution may offer unique features, desktop environments, and package management systems.

4. **Command Line and Graphical Interfaces:** While Linux provides powerful command-line interfaces for advanced users, it also offers user-friendly graphical interfaces for beginners. Desktop environments like GNOME, KDE Plasma, and XFCE provide visually intuitive ways to interact with the system.

5. **Package Management:** Linux distributions utilize package management systems to install, update, and remove software. This simplifies the process of installing applications and ensures a centralized method for managing software dependencies.

6. **Customization and Control:** Linux places customization at the forefront. Users have the freedom to tailor their desktop environments, themes, and applications according to their preferences. This empowers users to create an environment that suits their unique workflows.

7. **Stability and Security:** Linux is renowned for its stability and security. The collaborative nature of its development ensures that issues are addressed swiftly, while its architecture makes it inherently less susceptible to malware and viruses.

8. **Terminal and Shell**: Linux users have the option to work through the terminal—a text-based interface. This provides advanced users with powerful tools for system administration, scripting, and automation.

9. **Server and Embedded Systems:** Linux is not limited to personal computers. It is widely used as the foundation for servers, powering websites, cloud services, and networking equipment. It also thrives in embedded systems, found in devices like routers and IoT devices.

10. **Community and Support:** Linux's vibrant community fosters learning and collaboration. Online forums, documentation, and community-driven resources make it accessible to users of all levels.

11. **Regular Updates and Upgrades**: Linux distributions receive regular updates and upgrades to introduce new features, improvements, and security patches. This ensures that your system remains up to date and well-maintained.

Windows Computer to Buy

I recommended these windows computers for seniors due to their user-friendly interfaces and ease of use. Please note that availability and specifications may vary, so it's recommended to verify details before making a purchase:

Dell Inspiron 3000 Series Desktop ($349):

User-friendly interface with Windows 10

Suitable for basic tasks like browsing, email, and video calls

Affordable and straightforward design

Various configurations available based on needs

HP Pavilion All-in-One PC ($599):

All-in-one design for a clutter-free setup

Touchscreen option for intuitive navigation

Ideal for web browsing, video streaming, and light productivity tasks

Windows 10 for a familiar interface

Lenovo IdeaCentre AIO Desktop ($589):

Sleek all-in-one design

Clear display with adjustable screen sizes

User-friendly interface suitable for seniors

Multiple configurations to choose from

Acer Aspire TC Series Desktop ($779):

Affordable and reliable option

Straightforward setup and usage

Windows 10 for easy navigation

Suitable for internet browsing, email, and light tasks

Microsoft Surface Laptop:

Premium build quality and design

Lightweight and portable

Touchscreen display for intuitive interaction

Windows 10 provides a familiar environment

HP Envy x360 Convertible Laptop:

Convertible design for flexibility

Touchscreen functionality for ease of use

Suitable for browsing, video calls, and entertainment

Windows 10 with touch-friendly features

Dell Inspiron 14 Series Laptop:

Compact and lightweight design

Suitable for casual internet use and email

Windows 10 interface for simplicity

Multiple configurations available

Lenovo ThinkPad E Series Laptop:

Sturdy build and comfortable keyboard

Windows 10 for ease of use

Suitable for seniors who need a reliable laptop for tasks like email and document editing

Please note that the above list is based on general recommendations for seniors and their ease of use. Before making a purchase, it's advisable to consider the specific needs and preferences of the senior individual, as well as any required features like touchscreen functionality, screen size, and budget constraints.

How to Setup Your Computer

Here is a step-by-step guide on how to set up your windows computer:

Step 1: Unboxing and Inspection
Upon receiving your new computer, carefully unbox it and inspect the contents to ensure everything is included and undamaged. Typical items in the box include the computer itself, a power cord, a keyboard, a mouse (if not a laptop with a built-in touchpad), and documentation such as user manuals.

Step 2: Finding a Suitable Location
Choose an appropriate location for your computer. Ensure it's near an electrical outlet and provides good ventilation to prevent overheating. A comfortable chair and well-lit area are also important for extended computer use.

Step 3: Connecting Hardware
Power Supply: Plug the power cord into the computer and the electrical outlet. Ensure the computer is off before doing this.

Display: Connect the monitor to the computer using the appropriate cable (HDMI, VGA, DisplayPort, etc.). If it's an all-in-one PC or laptop, this step is unnecessary.

Keyboard and Mouse: If using a desktop PC, connect the keyboard and mouse to the appropriate USB ports.

External Devices: If you have external devices like speakers or a printer, connect them to the computer as needed.

Step 4: Turning On the Computer
Power Button: Locate the power button on your computer. It's often located on the front or top of the computer case for desktops, or near the keyboard for laptops.

Initial Setup: Press the power button to turn on the computer. Follow any on-screen instructions for initial setup, which may include selecting a language, time zone, and network connection. If you're prompted to connect to Wi-Fi, provide the network credentials (SSID and password).

Step 5: Setting Up Windows
User Account: Windows will ask you to create or sign in with a Microsoft account. If you don't have one, you can create a new account or use your computer offline with a local account.

Customize Settings: Choose your privacy and customization settings. You can adjust settings like whether to share data with Microsoft or customize the appearance of your desktop.

Create a PIN or Password: Set up a PIN or password to secure your computer. This is important for protecting your data.

Install Updates: Allow Windows to check for and install updates. This keeps your computer secure and up to date.

Step 6: Installing Software and Applications
Once Windows is set up, you can start installing the software and applications you need. This may include web browsers, email clients, office suites, and other tools. You can download software from the official websites or use the Microsoft Store for many applications.

Step 7: Personalizing Your Desktop

Customize your desktop by adding shortcuts to your favorite applications and organizing files into folders. You can also change your desktop background and screensaver by right-clicking on the desktop and selecting "Personalize."

Step 8: Configuring Additional Peripherals

If you have additional peripherals like a printer or external hard drive, follow the manufacturer's instructions to set them up. Windows should automatically detect many peripherals and install necessary drivers.

Step 9: Creating Backups

Creating backups is a crucial step to safeguard your important files and data from loss due to unforeseen events like hardware failure, accidental deletion, or data corruption. Here's a step-by-step guide on how to create backups on a Windows computer:

Step 1: Decide on a Backup Location

External Drive: Using an external hard drive or a USB flash drive is a convenient and cost-effective way to create backups. Purchase an external drive with sufficient storage capacity to accommodate your backup needs.

Network Attached Storage (NAS): If you have multiple computers on a network, consider using a NAS device. It provides centralized storage accessible by all networked devices.

Cloud Storage: Cloud services like Microsoft OneDrive, Google Drive, or Dropbox offer online backup solutions. These services provide storage in the cloud, allowing you to access your data from anywhere with an internet connection.

Step 2: Set Up Windows Backup

Open Settings: Click on the "Start" button, then select "Settings" (the gear-shaped icon).

Update & Security: In the Settings window, click on "Update & Security."

Backup: From the left sidebar, select "Backup."

Add a Drive: Under "Backup using File History," click on "Add a drive" and select your external drive or network location. If using a cloud service, configure it according to the service's instructions.

Step 3: Configure Backup Settings

Choose Folders: Click on "More options" under "Backup using File History." Here, you can choose which folders and libraries to include in the backup. You can also exclude specific folders if needed.

Backup Frequency: Adjust the frequency of backups. By default, Windows backs up files every hour. You can change this interval to daily or more frequently based on your preferences.

File Versions: Specify how long you want to keep saved versions of files. Windows can store previous versions of files for as long as you choose.

Step 4: Initiate the Backup

Start Backup: Once you've configured your backup settings, click on "Back up now." Windows will begin the initial backup, which may take some time, depending on the amount of data.

Automatic Backups: Subsequent backups will occur automatically according to your specified schedule. You can manually trigger a backup at any time by clicking "Back up now."

Step 5: Verify and Restore Backups

Verify Backup: Periodically check your backups to ensure they are functioning as expected. Access the "Backup options" in the Backup settings to confirm the last backup time and check for any errors.

Restore Files: In case of data loss or accidental deletion, you can restore files from your backup. Navigate to the folder or file you want to restore, right-click, and select "Restore previous versions." Windows will display available versions for restoration.

Step 6: Maintain Regular Backups

To ensure your data is always protected, maintain a regular backup schedule. Continue to monitor your backups, update settings as needed, and periodically test file restoration to ensure your data can be recovered when necessary.

By following these steps and maintaining regular backups, you can significantly reduce the risk of data loss and have peace of mind knowing your important files are secure.

Chapter 2

Learning the Basics

Knowing and Mastering Your Compter Keyboard

Mastering your computer keyboard is a valuable skill that can greatly enhance your efficiency and productivity while using a computer. Here's a step-by-step guide on how to become proficient in using your computer keyboard:

Step 1: Familiarize Yourself with the Keyboard Layout

Key Layout: Begin by familiarizing yourself with the layout of the keyboard. Most keyboards follow the QWERTY layout, which is the standard for English-language keyboards. Pay attention to the arrangement of letters, numbers, and special characters.

Function Keys: Identify the function keys (F1 through F12) located at the top of the keyboard. These keys have various purposes and can perform specific functions in different applications.

Step 2: Learn the Home Row Position

Home Row: Place your fingers on the "home row" keys. For the standard QWERTY layout, this includes the keys A, S, D, F, and J, K, L, and the semicolon (;). Your thumbs should rest on the spacebar.

Finger Placement: Assign each finger to specific keys. The left pinky covers the A key, and the right pinky covers the semicolon (;). The remaining fingers should be positioned accordingly.

Step 3: Practice Typing

Touch Typing: The key to keyboard mastery is touch typing. This means typing without looking at the keys. Practice typing words, sentences, and paragraphs repeatedly to build muscle memory.

Accuracy over Speed: Focus on accuracy before speed. Gradually increase your typing speed as your accuracy improves.

Step 4: Learn Common Shortcuts

Ctrl, Alt, and Shift: Familiarize yourself with the Ctrl (Control), Alt, and Shift keys. These modifier keys are used in combination with other keys to perform various functions, such as copying and pasting (Ctrl + C and Ctrl + V) or switching between open applications (Alt + Tab).

Windows Key: On Windows keyboards, the Windows key (usually adorned with the Windows logo) provides quick access to the Start menu and various shortcuts. Explore its functions.

Step 5: Explore Special Characters

Special Characters: Learn how to access special characters and symbols. This is especially useful for typing accented characters, currency symbols, and mathematical symbols. On Windows, you can use the "Alt" key in combination with numeric codes.

Character Map: On Windows, you can access the Character Map tool to find and insert special characters easily.

Step 6: Master Keyboard Shortcuts

Basic Shortcuts: Familiarize yourself with common keyboard shortcuts such as Ctrl + C (Copy), Ctrl + X (Cut), Ctrl + V (Paste), Ctrl + Z (Undo), and Ctrl + S (Save). These shortcuts are universally applicable in various applications.

Application-Specific Shortcuts: Different software applications have their own keyboard shortcuts. Explore these shortcuts in applications you frequently use, such as word processors, web browsers, and email clients.

Step 7: Practice Regularly

Daily Practice: Consistent practice is key to mastering the keyboard. Set aside time each day for typing exercises and practice.

Typing Games and Tutorials: Consider using online typing games and tutorials to improve your skills and increase your typing speed.

Step 8: Seek Feedback and Improvement

Typing Tests: Take online typing tests to measure your typing speed and accuracy regularly. Use the results to track your progress and identify areas for improvement.

Feedback: If possible, seek feedback from experienced typists or consider professional typing courses for more advanced skills.

Connecting your Computer to the Internet

Step 1: Ensure You Have the Necessary Equipment

Before connecting to the internet, make sure you have the following equipment ready:

Computer: Ensure your computer is in working order and powered on.

Modem: If you have a DSL or cable internet connection, you will need a modem. For fiber-optic or other types of connections, a modem or ONT (Optical Network Terminal) may be provided by your internet service provider (ISP).

Router: A router is essential for creating a local network in your home or office. It allows multiple devices to connect to the internet through a single internet connection.

Ethernet Cable: You'll need an Ethernet cable (also known as a network cable) to connect your computer to the router or modem. Alternatively, you can use a wireless connection if your computer has Wi-Fi capabilities.

Internet Service Plan: You must have an active internet service plan with an ISP. Ensure your account is in good standing and that you have the necessary credentials to connect.

Step 2: Connect the Hardware

Modem Setup:
Plug the modem into a power outlet and turn it on if it has a power switch.

Connect one end of the Ethernet cable to the modem's Ethernet port.

Connect the other end of the Ethernet cable to the WAN or Internet port on your router, if you have one.

Router Setup:
Plug the router into a power outlet and turn it on.

Connect your computer to one of the router's LAN ports using another Ethernet cable.

Step 3: Configure the Router

Access the Router's Configuration Page:

Open a web browser on your computer.

In the address bar, type the router's IP address. Common router IP addresses are 192.168.0.1 or 192.168.1.1. You can find the IP address in the router's user manual or on a sticker on the router itself.

Log in to the router's configuration page using the administrator credentials. These are often found on a sticker on the router or in the router's manual.

Set Up Wireless (Wi-Fi):
If your router supports Wi-Fi and you want to use a wireless connection, configure the Wi-Fi settings, including the network name (SSID) and password (Wi-Fi key). This step is optional if you plan to use a wired Ethernet connection.

Step 4: Test the Connection

Restart Modem and Router:

Once you've configured your router, restart both the modem and the router. This can help ensure a stable connection.

Connect Your Computer:

Ensure your computer is connected to the router either via Ethernet cable or Wi-Fi.

Test the Connection:

Open a web browser and try accessing a website to confirm that your computer is connected to the internet.

Troubleshooting (if needed)
If you encounter connectivity issues, consider the following troubleshooting steps:

Restart Devices: Try restarting your modem, router, and computer.

Check Cables: Ensure all cables are securely connected.

Contact Your ISP: If you can't resolve the issue, contact your internet service provider for assistance.

The Desktop of Your Computer System

The desktop of a computer's operating system serves as the user's primary workspace, allowing easy access to files, folders, applications, and shortcuts. Here, we'll explore everything you need to know about the desktop, including creating folders and managing icons:

Desktop Icons:

Icons represent various elements such as files, folders, and applications.

By default, you might find icons for the Recycle Bin (Windows) or Trash (macOS) and possibly shortcuts to commonly used applications.

Wallpaper/Background:

The background or wallpaper is the visual backdrop of your desktop.

You can personalize it by right-clicking on an empty area of the desktop and selecting "Personalize" (Windows) or "Change Desktop Background" (macOS) to choose from a selection of images or use your own.

Creating Folders:

Windows:

To create a new folder on the desktop, right-click on an empty area.

Hover over "New" and select "Folder."

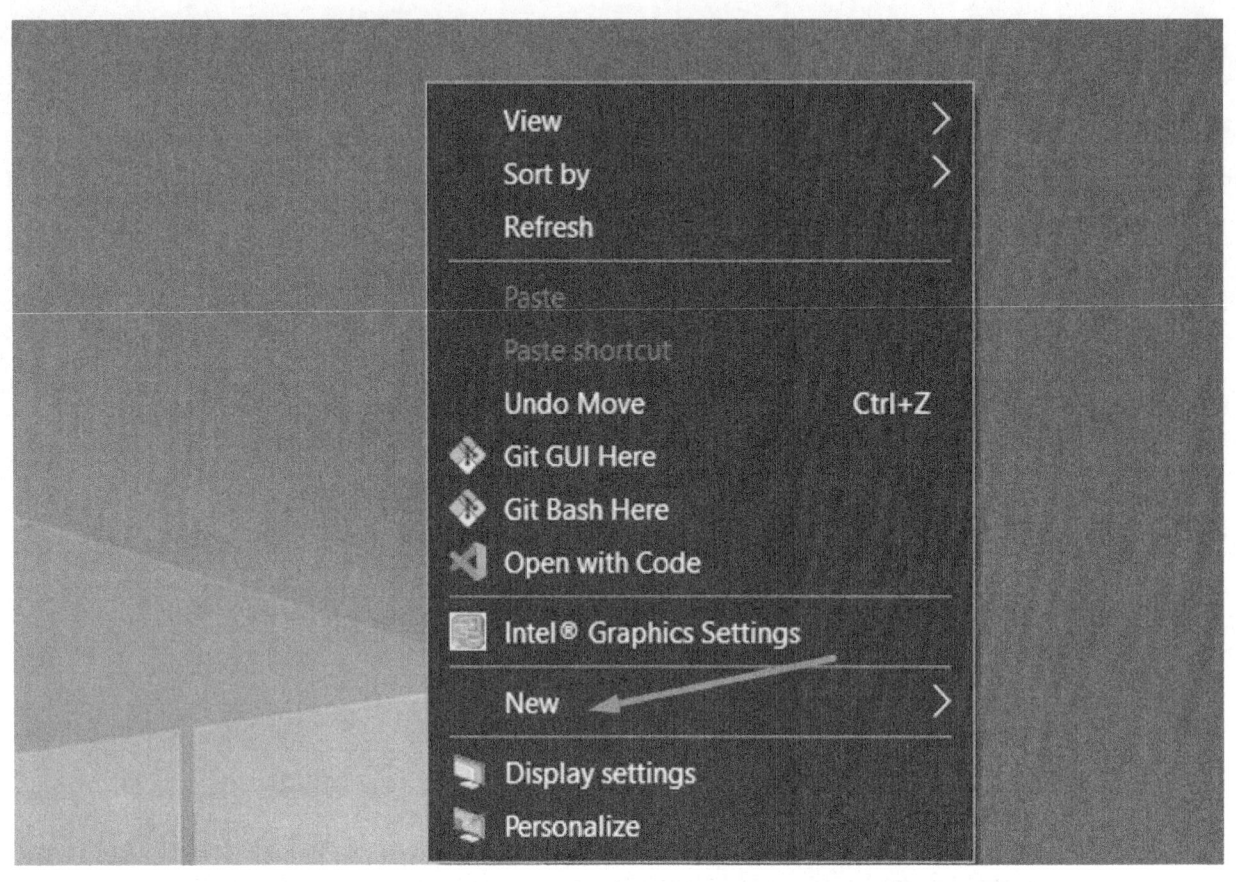

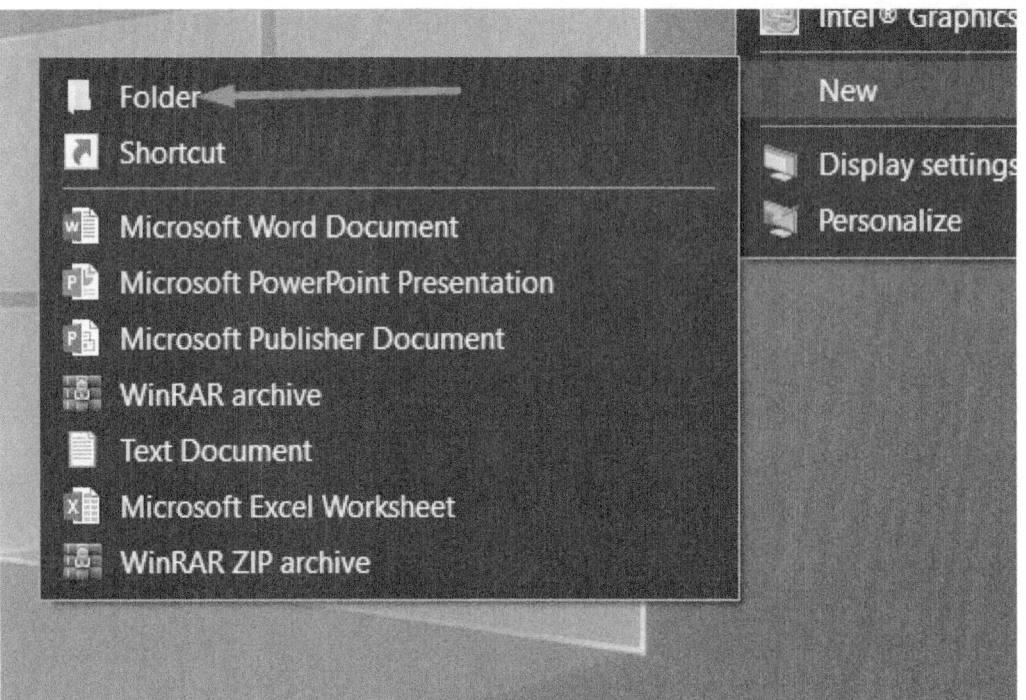

Rename the folder by right-clicking and selecting "Rename."

macOS:

To create a folder, click anywhere on the desktop to ensure you're not in an active window.

Go to the "File" menu and select "New Folder" or use the keyboard shortcut Shift + Command + N.

Rename the folder by clicking on its name.

Moving and Organizing Icons:

Windows:

To move an icon, click and drag it to a new location on the desktop.

To organize icons, right-click on the desktop and choose "Sort by." You can sort by name, size, item type, or date modified.

macOS:

To move an icon, click and drag it to a new location.

To arrange icons, right-click on the desktop and select "Clean Up By" to sort by name, kind, date, or label.

Creating Shortcuts:

Windows:

You can create shortcuts to applications or files by right-clicking the item, selecting "Send to," and choosing "Desktop (create shortcut)."

Alternatively, drag and drop an application or file onto the desktop while holding down the right mouse button. Release the button and choose "Create shortcuts here."

macOS:

Create an alias (shortcut) by selecting an application or file and going to "File" > "Make Alias" or using the keyboard shortcut Command + L.

Drag the alias to the desktop.

Deleting Icons:

Windows:

To delete an icon, right-click on it and select "Delete."

Alternatively, drag the icon to the Recycle Bin.

macOS:

To delete an icon, click on it to select it and then press the "Delete" key or drag it to the Trash.

Restoring Deleted Items:

Windows:

Deleted items go to the Recycle Bin. To restore an item, open the Recycle Bin, right-click on the item, and select "Restore."

macOS:

Deleted items go to the Trash. To restore an item, open the Trash, drag the item to the desktop or another location.

The desktop is a versatile workspace for managing files, folders, and shortcuts. Organizing it efficiently can improve your productivity and make accessing your most-used items quick and convenient.

Chapter 3

Working with Applications

Installing New Applications:

Step 1: Downloading the Application:

Windows:

- Open your web browser and go to the official website of the application you want to download.
- Look for a "Download" or "Get" button on the website and click it.
- Follow the on-screen instructions to download the installation file (usually a .exe file).

macOS:

- Visit the official website of the application you want to download using your web browser.
- Look for a "Download" button or link and click it.
- macOS will typically download a .dmg or .pkg file. Locate the downloaded file in your Downloads folder.

Step 2: Installing the Application:

Windows:

Locate the downloaded installation file (usually in the Downloads folder) and double-click it.

Follow the on-screen prompts to install the application. This typically involves accepting the terms of use, choosing an installation location, and clicking "Install."

macOS:

- Locate the downloaded .dmg or .pkg file in your Downloads folder and double-click it.
- A new window will appear. Drag the application icon to the "Applications" folder to install it. macOS will copy the application to the Applications folder.

Accessing Installed Applications

Step 1: Accessing Applications (Windows):

From the Start Menu:

- Click on the "Start" button (Windows logo) in the lower-left corner of the screen.
- A menu will appear with a list of installed applications. You can scroll through and click on the application you want to open.
- Using the Search Bar (Windows):
- Type the name of the application you want to open in the search bar next to the Start button.
- Windows will display a list of matching applications. Click on the one you want to open.

Step 2: Accessing Applications (macOS)

From the Dock:

- The Dock is a bar at the bottom (or side) of your screen that contains icons of frequently used applications.
- Click on an icon in the Dock to open the associated application.
- From the Applications Folder:
- Click on the "Finder" icon in the Dock (usually looks like a blue face).
- In the Finder window, click on "Applications" in the sidebar.
- Locate the application you want to open and double-click it.

Chapter 4

Staying Safe Online

Internet security basics are crucial for anyone using the internet, as they help protect individuals and their data from various online threats.

Understanding Internet Security

Internet security refers to a set of measures taken to ensure the protection of data, information, and systems while connected to the internet.

The goal is to prevent unauthorized access, data breaches, identity theft, and other cybercrimes.

Common Threats:

Malware

Malicious software, including viruses, worms, trojans, and spyware, designed to harm or exploit computers and networks.

Phishing

Deceptive attempts to obtain sensitive information by posing as a trustworthy entity.

Cyberattacks

Deliberate and targeted attempts to compromise the integrity, confidentiality, or availability of information.

Antivirus and Anti-malware Software

Antivirus and anti-malware programs are essential tools for preventing, detecting, and removing malicious software.

Regularly update these programs to ensure they have the latest virus definitions and security patches.

Firewalls:

Firewalls act as a barrier between your computer and potential threats from the internet.

They monitor and control incoming and outgoing network traffic based on predetermined security rules.

Secure Browsing Practices:

HTTPS: Ensure websites use HTTPS (secure protocol) for encrypted communication, especially when entering sensitive information like passwords or credit card details.

Avoiding Suspicious Links: Be cautious when clicking on links in emails or on websites, particularly if they seem unexpected or untrustworthy.

Regular Software Updates:

Keep the operating system, antivirus software, web browsers, and other applications up to date with the latest security patches.

Software updates often include fixes for vulnerabilities that could be exploited by cybercriminals.

Password Management:
Use strong, unique passwords for each online account.

Consider using a password manager to generate and store complex passwords securely.

Two-Factor Authentication (2FA):
Enable 2FA whenever possible to add an extra layer of security beyond just a password.

This typically involves receiving a code on a secondary device or through a separate authentication app.

Safe Email Practices:

Avoid opening emails from unknown senders or clicking on suspicious attachments or links.

Verify the legitimacy of unexpected emails, especially those requesting sensitive information.

Network Security
Use a secure and encrypted Wi-Fi connection, and change default router passwords.

Consider using a virtual private network (VPN) for additional privacy and security when accessing the internet.

Data Backups

Regularly back up important data to an external drive or cloud service to mitigate the impact of potential data loss due to cyberattacks or hardware failures.

Chapter 5

Basic Troubleshooting

Basic troubleshooting for Windows and macOS involves identifying and resolving common issues that users may encounter. Here's a guide for both operating systems:

Windows

1. Slow Performance:

- Check Disk Space: Ensure that there is sufficient free space on the hard drive.
- Disable Startup Programs: Use the Task Manager to disable unnecessary programs that launch at startup.
- Scan for Malware: Run a full antivirus scan to check for malware.

2. Error Messages:

- Google the Error: Search for the exact error message online to find potential solutions.
- Check Event Viewer: Use the Event Viewer to review system and application logs for error details.
- Update Drivers: Ensure that device drivers are up to date.

3. Software Updates:

- Windows Update: Ensure that Windows is set to automatically install updates.
- Update Applications: Keep third-party applications updated to the latest versions.

4. Back Up Your Data:

- Regular Backups: Set up regular backups of important files using built-in tools or third-party software.
- Create a System Restore Point: Before making significant changes, create a system restore point for easy recovery.

5. Internet Connection Issues:

- Restart Router: Power cycle the router to resolve connectivity issues.
- Check Network Settings: Verify that network settings are correctly configured.
- Update Network Drivers: Ensure that network drivers are up to date.

macOS:

1. Slow Performance:

- Check Disk Space: Ensure sufficient free space on the hard drive.
- Activity Monitor: Use Activity Monitor to identify resource-intensive processes.
- Clear Cache and Temporary Files: Remove unnecessary cache and temporary files.

2. Error Messages:

- Console App: Use the Console app to view system logs for error messages.
- Verify Disk: Use Disk Utility to check and repair disk permissions and errors.
- Safe Mode: Boot into Safe Mode to troubleshoot issues caused by third-party applications.

3. Software Updates:

- App Store: Update macOS and installed applications from the App Store.
- Terminal Updates: Use Terminal commands for system updates if needed.

4. Back Up Your Data:

- Time Machine: Set up Time Machine for automatic backups.
- External Drive Backups: Manually copy important files to an external drive.

5. Internet Connection Issues:

- Restart Router: Power cycle the router to resolve connectivity issues.
- Network Preferences: Check network settings in System Preferences.
- Renew DHCP Lease: Use the Network Utility to renew the DHCP lease.

- General Tips for Both Windows and macOS:

Restart Your Computer:

- A simple restart can resolve many temporary issues.

Check for Viruses and Malware:

- Run a full system scan using your antivirus software.

Check for Updates:

- Keep your operating system, drivers, and applications up to date.

Verify Hardware Connections:

- Ensure that all cables and hardware components are securely connected.

Review Recent Changes:

- If the issue started after a recent change, such as installing new software, consider reverting those changes.

Chapter 6

Introduction to Social Media

Facebook:

Facebook:

Creating an Account:

1. **Visit the Facebook Sign-Up Page:**

    - Go to Facebook.
    - Click on "Create New Account."

2. **Provide Information:**

    - Enter your name, email or mobile number, password, date of birth, and gender.
    - Click "Sign Up."

3. **Confirm Your Email or Mobile Number:**

    - Follow the prompts to confirm your email or mobile number.

Managing Your Account:

1. **Profile Setup:**

    - Add a profile picture and cover photo.
    - Complete your profile details, such as education, work, and hometown.

2. **Privacy Settings:**

    - Adjust your privacy settings to control who can see your posts and personal information.

3. **Connecting with Friends:**

    - Find and connect with friends by searching for their names or importing contacts.

4. **Posting and Interacting:**
   - Share updates, photos, and videos.
   - Like, comment, and share content from others.

2. X (Twitter):

Creating an Account:

1. **Visit the Twitter Sign-Up Page:**
   - Go to [Twitter](#).
   - Click on "Sign Up."

2. **Provide Information:**
   - Enter your name, email or mobile number, and password.
   - Click "Sign up for Twitter."

3. **Choose a Username:**
   - Pick a unique username that represents you.

Managing Your Account:

1. **Profile Setup:**
   - Add a profile picture, header image, and bio.
   - Customize your profile with your interests and website link.

2. **Follow and Be Followed:**
   - Follow accounts of interest.
   - Gain followers by sharing interesting content.

3. **Tweeting and Interacting:**
   - Tweet text, photos, and videos.
   - Like, retweet, and reply to other users' tweets.

3. LinkedIn:

Creating an Account:

1. **Visit the LinkedIn Sign-Up Page:**
   - Go to LinkedIn.
   - Click on "Join now."

2. **Provide Information:**
   - Enter your first and last name, email, and password.
   - Click "Join now."

3. **Profile Setup:**
   - Add a professional photo and headline.
   - Fill in your work experience, education, and skills.

Managing Your Account:

1. **Connections:**
   - Connect with colleagues, classmates, and professionals in your industry.

2. **Engagement:**
   - Share updates, articles, and insights.
   - Engage with others by commenting and liking their posts.

3. **Groups and Networking:**
   - Join LinkedIn Groups related to your field.
   - Attend networking events and connect with professionals.

4. Instagram:

Creating an Account:

1. **Download the Instagram App:**

- Install the app from the App Store (iOS) or Google Play Store (Android).

2. **Sign Up:**
    - Open the app and sign up with your email or phone number.

3. **Create a Username and Password:**
    - Choose a unique username and set a password.

Managing Your Account:

1. **Profile Setup:**
    - Add a profile picture, bio, and website link.
    - Connect your account to Facebook for cross-posting.

2. **Posting Content:**
    - Share photos and videos on your profile.
    - Use hashtags to increase visibility.

3. **Interacting:**
    - Follow other users and be followed.
    - Like, comment, and direct message other users.

Privacy Settings

Managing privacy settings is crucial to control the visibility of your personal information and activities on social media platforms. Below are general guidelines on adjusting privacy settings on popular platforms like Facebook, Twitter, LinkedIn, and Instagram:

1. Facebook:

Adjusting Privacy Settings:

Profile Privacy:

Click on the down arrow in the top right corner.

- Go to "Settings & Privacy" > "Settings."
- Navigate to "Privacy" in the left sidebar.
- Adjust settings for who can see your future posts, who can send you friend requests, and more.

Timeline and Tagging:

- Under "Settings & Privacy," go to "Settings."
- Navigate to "Timeline and Tagging."
- Adjust settings for who can post on your timeline, who can tag you, and more.

Apps and Websites:

- Go to "Settings & Privacy" > "Settings."
- Select "Apps and Websites" to review and control third-party app access.

2. X(Twitter):

Adjusting Privacy Settings:

Tweet Privacy:

- Click on your profile picture in the top right.
- Go to "Settings and privacy."
- Navigate to "Privacy and safety."
- Adjust settings for tweet privacy, including who can see your tweets and who can tag you in photos.

Account Privacy:

- Under "Privacy and safety," adjust settings for who can follow you and who can send you direct messages.

3. LinkedIn:

Adjusting Privacy Settings:

Profile Privacy:

- Click on your profile picture.
- Go to "Settings & Privacy."
- Navigate to "Visibility" to control who can see your connections, activity feed, and more.

Activity Broadcasts:

- In "Settings & Privacy," go to "Privacy" > "How others see your LinkedIn activity."
- Adjust settings for activity broadcasts and notifications.
- Profile Viewing Options:
- Under "Privacy," go to "Profile viewing options."
- Choose whether to show your name and headline when viewing other profiles.

4. Instagram:

Adjusting Privacy Settings:

Account Privacy:

- Open the Instagram app.
- Go to your profile and tap on the three lines in the top right.
- Navigate to "Settings" > "Privacy."
- Adjust settings for account privacy, including who can see your posts and who can send you messages.

Activity Status:

- In "Privacy," adjust settings for who can see your activity status.

Story Controls:

- Under "Privacy," go to "Story."

- Adjust settings for who can see your stories and who can reply to them.

Connecting with Friends and Family

Connecting with friends and family on social media platforms is a common and enjoyable way to stay in touch and share experiences. Below are general guidelines on how to connect with others on popular social media platforms like Facebook, Twitter, LinkedIn, and Instagram:

1. Facebook:

Sending Friend Requests:

1. **Search for Friends:**
    - Use the search bar to find friends by name or email.
    - Browse suggested friends based on mutual connections.

2. **Send Friend Requests:**
    - Visit the profile of the person you want to connect with.
    - Click the "Add Friend" button.
    - Wait for the friend request to be accepted.

Managing Friend Requests:

1. **Accepting Requests:**
    - If someone sends you a friend request, you'll receive a notification.
    - Click "Confirm" to accept the request.

2. **Rejecting Requests:**
    - If you don't want to connect with someone, click "Delete Request."

2. Twitter:

Following Others:

1. **Search for Accounts:**
   - Use the search bar to find friends and family members.
   - Look for their Twitter handles or names.

2. **Follow Accounts:**
   - Visit the profile of the person you want to follow.
   - Click the "Follow" button.
   - Wait for them to follow you back for mutual connections.

Managing Followers:

1. **Accepting Followers:**
   - Twitter is an open platform, and users can follow you without approval.
   - You can set your account to private to control who follows you.

3. LinkedIn:

Connecting with Professionals:

1. **Search for Connections:**
   - Use the search bar to find colleagues, classmates, and professionals.
   - Connect with people you know or those in your industry.

2. **Send Connection Requests:**
   - Visit the profile of the person you want to connect with.
   - Click the "Connect" button.
   - Add a personalized message if desired.

Managing Connections:

1. **Accepting Requests:**

- If someone sends you a connection request, you'll receive a notification.
- Click "Accept" to connect with them.

2. **Removing Connections:**
    - If you want to disconnect from someone, go to their profile and click "More" > "Remove Connection."

4. Instagram:

Following Others:

1. **Search for Accounts:**
    - Use the search bar to find friends, family, or accounts of interest.

2. **Follow Accounts:**
    - Visit the profile of the person you want to follow.
    - Click the "Follow" button.

Managing Followers:

1. **Accepting Followers:**
    - Instagram is an open platform, and users can follow you without approval.
    - You can set your account to private to control who follows you.

2. **Removing Followers:**
    - If you want to remove a follower, go to their profile, click "Following," and then click "Remove."

Chapter 7

Exploring Multimedia

Understanding Multimedia

This involves grasping the use of multiple forms of media, such as text, graphics, audio, video, and interactive elements, to convey information and engage users. Multimedia is widely used across various platforms, including websites, presentations, educational materials, and entertainment content.

Key Components of Multimedia:

1. **Text:**
    - Traditional written content remains a vital component of multimedia, providing context, explanations, and information.

2. **Graphics and Images:**
    - Visual elements, including images, illustrations, charts, and graphs, enhance the visual appeal and understanding of content.

3. **Audio:**
    - Sound elements, including music, narration, and sound effects, contribute to the auditory experience and can convey emotions or enhance storytelling.

4. **Video:**
    - Moving images, animations, and video clips are powerful tools for conveying complex information, demonstrating processes, or telling stories.

5. **Interactive Elements:**
    - Multimedia can involve interactive features such as buttons, links, quizzes, and user interfaces, allowing users to engage actively with the content.

Concepts and Considerations:

1. **Integration:**

- Effective multimedia integrates different elements seamlessly to create a cohesive and engaging user experience.

2. **User Experience (UX):**
    - Design considerations, including layout, navigation, and aesthetics, are crucial for a positive user experience.

3. **Accessibility:**
    - Designing multimedia with accessibility in mind ensures that content is usable by people with disabilities, incorporating features like alt text for images and captions for videos.

4. **Storytelling:**
    - Multimedia is often used as a storytelling tool, combining various elements to create a narrative that resonates with the audience.

5. **Bandwidth and Loading Times:**
    - Consideration of file sizes and media compression is essential, particularly for online platforms, to optimize loading times and accommodate varying internet speeds.

6. **Interactivity and Engagement:**
    - Interactive multimedia engages users, encouraging participation and enhancing the learning or entertainment experience.

Use Cases:

1. **Educational Multimedia:**
    - Multimedia is extensively used in educational settings, offering dynamic learning materials, interactive lessons, and simulations.

2. **Entertainment Industry:**
    - Films, video games, and music videos are prime examples of multimedia in the entertainment industry, combining audio, visual, and interactive elements.

3. **Web Design:**

- Websites often incorporate multimedia to create engaging and visually appealing user interfaces, including images, videos, and interactive features.

4. **Marketing and Advertising:**
    - Multimedia plays a crucial role in marketing, where engaging visuals, videos, and interactive content are used to attract and retain audience attention.

5. **Presentations:**
    - Multimedia is frequently employed in presentations to convey information more dynamically, using visuals, audio, and video to enhance audience understanding.

Photos and Images

Photos and images are visual elements that play a crucial role in conveying information, expressing emotions, and enhancing communication across various mediums. Whether used for personal enjoyment, educational purposes, or in professional settings, photos and images are powerful tools for storytelling and visual representation. Here's an overview of key concepts related to photos and images:

Types of Images:

1. **Photographs:**
    - Captured using cameras, photographs are realistic representations of scenes or subjects.

2. **Illustrations:**
    - Created by artists, illustrations are often drawn or digitally rendered and can range from simple diagrams to intricate artwork.

3. **Graphics:**
    - Graphical elements include charts, graphs, icons, and symbols used to represent data or convey specific concepts.

4. **Infographics:**
    - Infographics combine text and visuals, presenting information in a visually appealing and easy-to-understand format.

Key Concepts:

1. **Resolution:**
    - The clarity and detail of an image are determined by its resolution, measured in pixels. Higher resolution generally results in sharper images.

2. **Aspect Ratio:**
    - The proportional relationship between an image's width and height. Different aspect ratios are suitable for various purposes, such as social media posts, print materials, or widescreen presentations.

3. **File Formats:**
    - Common image file formats include JPEG, PNG, GIF, and TIFF. Each format has its characteristics, advantages, and best use cases.

4. **Editing and Manipulation:**
    - Photo editing tools allow for adjustments in brightness, contrast, color balance, and cropping. Advanced tools like Adobe Photoshop enable more intricate manipulations.

5. **Copyright and Licensing:**
    - Understanding copyright laws and licensing is crucial when using images. Ensure that you have the right to use an image for your intended purpose.

Uses of Photos and Images:

1. **Visual Storytelling:**
   - Images are powerful tools for conveying narratives, evoking emotions, and telling stories in a compelling way.

2. **Branding and Marketing:**
   - Companies use images to build brand identity, create marketing materials, and engage with their audience through visually appealing content.

3. **Educational Materials:**
   - Images are extensively used in textbooks, presentations, and e-learning materials to enhance understanding and retention of information.

4. **Web Design:**
   - Websites use images to create visually appealing layouts, convey information, and improve user experience.

5. **Social Media:**
   - Social media platforms rely heavily on images for user engagement. Posts with captivating visuals tend to attract more attention.

Best Practices:

1. **High-Quality Images:**
   - Use high-resolution images for clarity and visual appeal.

2. **Consistency:**
   - Maintain a consistent visual style across your images for a cohesive presentation.

3. **Relevance:**
   - Ensure that images are relevant to the content they accompany.

4. **Alt Text:**
   - Include descriptive alt text with images, especially on websites, for accessibility and SEO purposes.

5. **Optimization:**
   - Optimize image file sizes for faster loading times on websites without compromising quality.

Music & Videos

Music and videos are powerful forms of multimedia that entertain, communicate, and evoke emotions. Whether used for artistic expression, entertainment, or educational purposes, music and videos play a significant role in our daily lives. Here's an overview of key concepts related to music and videos:

Music:

1. **Genres:**
   - Music is classified into various genres based on styles, themes, and cultural influences. Common genres include pop, rock, hip-hop, classical, jazz, and more.

2. **Composition Elements:**
   - **Melody:** The sequence of single pitches forming a musical phrase.
   - **Harmony:** The combination of different musical notes played simultaneously.
   - **Rhythm:** The pattern of beats and timing in music.
   - **Lyrics:** Words or text sung by the vocalist.

3. **Musical Instruments:**
   - A wide array of instruments is used to create music, including string instruments (guitar, violin), wind instruments (flute, saxophone),

percussion instruments (drums, tambourine), and keyboard instruments (piano, organ).

4. **Production and Recording:**
   - Modern music often involves digital recording and production techniques using software and hardware to enhance and manipulate sounds.

5. **Distribution Platforms:**
   - Music can be distributed through various platforms, including streaming services (Spotify, Apple Music), digital downloads (iTunes), and physical formats (CDs, vinyl).

6. **Live Performances:**
   - Musicians often perform live in concerts, festivals, and other events, connecting directly with their audience.

Videos:

1. **Genres and Formats:**
   - Videos come in various genres, including movies, TV shows, documentaries, music videos, and short films. Formats include live-action, animation, and a combination of both.

2. **Storyboarding:**
   - Before production, videos are often planned through storyboarding, a sequence of illustrations or images that represent key scenes.

3. **Cinematography:**
   - Cinematography involves camera work, composition, lighting, and other visual elements to create aesthetically pleasing and meaningful shots.

4. **Editing:**
   - Video editing involves assembling recorded footage, adding special effects, transitions, and sound to create a cohesive and engaging final product.

5. Distribution Platforms:

- Videos can be distributed through traditional methods such as TV and theaters, as well as through online platforms like YouTube, Netflix, Hulu, and other streaming services.

6. Virtual and Augmented Reality (VR/AR):

- Emerging technologies enable immersive video experiences, allowing users to interact with and explore virtual environments.

Best Practices:

1. **Quality Production:**
   - Both music and videos benefit from high-quality production techniques to enhance the overall experience.

2. **Storytelling:**
   - Effective storytelling in videos and meaningful lyrics in music contribute to audience engagement and emotional connection.

3. **Accessibility:**
   - Consideration for accessibility features, such as subtitles for videos and lyrics for music, ensures a wider audience can enjoy the content.

4. **Legal and Copyright Considerations:**
   - Respecting copyright laws and obtaining the necessary permissions for using music and videos is crucial.

5. **Adaptability:**
   - Considering the diverse preferences and devices of the audience ensures that content can be enjoyed across various platforms and contexts.

Managing and Enjoying Multimedia Content

Managing and enjoying multimedia content involves organizing, accessing, and experiencing a diverse range of media, including music, videos, images, and more. Here's a guide on how to effectively manage and enjoy multimedia content:

1. Organizing Multimedia Libraries:

Music:

1. **Use Playlists:**

    - Create playlists based on genres, moods, or activities to easily access preferred music.

2. **Metadata Management:**

    - Ensure that music files have accurate metadata (song title, artist, album) for easy navigation.

3. **Folder Organization:**

    - Organize music files into folders by artist or genre to streamline the library.

Videos:

1. **Create Folders:**

    - Organize videos into folders based on genres, TV shows, or movies.

2. **Use Streaming Playlists:**

    - Utilize streaming platforms with personalized playlists for easy access to recommended content.

3. **Metadata and Subtitles:**

    - Ensure that video files have accurate metadata and download subtitles for non-native language content.

Images:

1. **Tagging and Keywords:**
   - Use tags and keywords to categorize and quickly find images.

2. **Folder Organization:**
   - Organize images into folders by date, event, or theme.

3. **Cloud Storage:**
   - Consider cloud storage for backing up and accessing images across devices.

2. Digital Media Players and Platforms:

Music:

1. **Streaming Services:**
   - Use music streaming services like Spotify, Apple Music, or Deezer for a vast library and personalized recommendations.

2. **Local Media Players:**
   - Explore local media players like VLC or iTunes for managing offline music collections.

Videos:

1. **Streaming Platforms:**
   - Access video content through popular streaming platforms like Netflix, Hulu, or YouTube.

2. **Media Players:**
   - Use media players like VLC, Plex, or Kodi to manage and play local video files.

Images:

1. **Photo Management Apps:**
   - Use photo management apps like Google Photos or Adobe Lightroom for easy access and editing.

2. **Cloud Services:**
   - Upload and organize images in cloud services like Google Drive or Dropbox.

3. Personalization and Discovery:

1. **Curated Playlists:**
   - Explore curated playlists on music streaming platforms for new music recommendations.

2. **Recommendation Algorithms:**
   - Allow platforms to use recommendation algorithms to suggest movies, TV shows, or music based on preferences.

3. **Themed Playlists:**
   - Create themed playlists for different moods or occasions to enhance the listening or viewing experience.

4. Cross-Device Synchronization:

1. **Cloud Storage:**
   - Use cloud storage services to sync multimedia libraries across multiple devices.

2. **Streaming Services:**
   - Opt for streaming services that offer cross-device synchronization of playlists and preferences.

5. Optimizing Multimedia Experience:

1. **High-Quality Playback:**
   - Opt for high-quality playback settings on streaming platforms for an enhanced experience.

2. **Surround Sound and Headphones:**
   - Invest in quality audio equipment for an immersive music experience and consider using headphones for detailed audio.

3. **Screen Quality:**
   - Ensure optimal screen quality and resolution for an immersive video and image viewing experience.

6. Legal Considerations:

1. **Subscription Services:**
   - Subscribe to legal and licensed streaming services to access a vast library of content.

2. **Copyright Awareness:**
   - Be aware of copyright laws and respect intellectual property rights when sharing or using multimedia content.

Organizing Photo Albums

Organizing photo albums is a great way to keep your digital or physical photo collection structured, easily accessible, and enjoyable to browse. Here are some tips for organizing photo albums effectively:

Digital Photo Albums:

1. **Folder Structure:**
   - Create a logical and hierarchical folder structure. For example, you might have main folders for each year, and within each year, subfolders for events or months.

2. **Date-Based Organization:**
   - Organize photos chronologically based on the date they were taken or the event date.

3. **Event or Theme Folders:**
   - Create separate folders for specific events, occasions, or themes. For example, you might have folders for vacations, birthdays, or holidays.

4. **Use Descriptive Filenames:**

- Give your photos descriptive filenames that provide information about the content. This can be especially helpful for search purposes.

5. **Metadata Tags:**

    - Take advantage of metadata tags to add keywords, location information, and other relevant details to your photos. This can aid in searching and categorizing.

6. **Cloud Storage:**

    - Consider using cloud storage services that offer automatic photo organization and syncing across devices.

7. **Albums on Social Media:**

    - Utilize albums or collections on social media platforms to organize and share photos with friends and family.

8. **Backup Regularly:**

    - Regularly back up your photo collection to prevent loss in case of device failure. Cloud services and external hard drives are good options.

9. **Photo Management Software:**

    - Use photo management software like Adobe Lightroom, Google Photos, or Apple Photos for advanced organization and editing features.

10. **Face Recognition:**

    - Some photo management tools offer face recognition features, allowing you to easily tag and find photos of specific individuals.

Physical Photo Albums:

1. **Chronological Order:**

    - Arrange printed photos in chronological order within physical albums.

2. **Labeling:**
    - Label each photo with the date, location, and names of individuals if applicable. Use acid-free, archival-safe labels and pens.
3. **Dividers:**
    - Use dividers to separate different events or time periods within a physical album.
4. **Theme-Based Albums:**
    - Create themed albums for specific occasions, such as vacations, weddings, or family gatherings.
5. **Storage Conditions:**
    - Store physical albums in a cool, dry place away from direct sunlight to preserve the quality of the photos.
6. **Scrapbooking:**
    - Consider adding embellishments, captions, and notes to your physical albums for a personalized touch.
7. **Digitizing:**
    - Consider digitizing your physical photo collection to have a backup and to easily share with others.
8. **Album Preservation:**
    - Invest in high-quality, acid-free photo albums and storage materials to prevent deterioration over time.

Playing Music and Videos

Playing music and videos can be done through various devices and platforms, ranging from smartphones and computers to dedicated media players and smart TVs. Below are general steps for playing music and videos on different platforms:

Playing Music:

1. **Smartphones and Tablets:**

    - **iOS (iPhone and iPad):**

        1. Open the "Music" app.
        2. Browse or search for the desired song or album.
        3. Tap on the play button.

    - **Android:**

        1. Open the "Google Play Music" or "YouTube Music" app.
        2. Find and select the music you want to play.
        3. Tap the play button.

2. **Computers:**

    - **Windows:**

        1. Use a media player like Windows Media Player or VLC.
        2. Open the player, navigate to your music library, and double-click on the song you want to play.

    - **Mac:**

        1. Use the "Music" app or another third-party player like VLC.
        2. Open the app, find your music, and click the play button.

3. **Smart Speakers:**

    - **Amazon Echo (Alexa):**

        1. Say "Alexa, play [song/artist/genre]."

2. Alexa will find and play the requested music.

- **Google Home:**

    1. Say "Hey Google, play [song/artist/playlist]."

    2. Google Assistant will start playing the requested music.

Playing Videos:

1. **Smartphones and Tablets:**

   - **iOS (iPhone and iPad):**

       1. Open the "TV" app or the app associated with the video content.

       2. Browse or search for the video and tap play.

   - **Android:**

       1. Use video apps like YouTube or your device's built-in video player.

       2. Find and tap on the video you want to play.

2. **Computers:**

   - **Windows:**

       1. Use a media player like VLC or Windows Media Player.

       2. Open the player, navigate to your video, and click play.

   - **Mac:**

       1. Use the "TV" app or VLC for videos.

       2. Open the app, find your video, and click play.

3. **Smart TVs:**

   - **Streaming Apps:**

       1. Open the streaming app on your smart TV (e.g., Netflix, Hulu, YouTube).

       2. Browse or search for the video and select it to start playing.

   - **Casting/Mirroring:**

1. Use casting or screen mirroring features on your phone or computer to display content on the TV.

Tips:

1. **Playlists:**
   - Create playlists for music or video content to enjoy a curated sequence of content.

2. **Voice Commands:**
   - Many devices support voice commands, allowing you to control playback with your voice.

3. **Streaming Services:**
   - Subscribe to streaming services for access to a vast library of music and video content.

4. **Offline Playback:**
   - Download music and videos for offline playback when an internet connection is not available.

5. **Quality Settings:**
   - Adjust video quality settings based on your internet speed to avoid buffering.

Chapter 8

Microsoft Word
Getting Started with Microsoft Word

Overview of Microsoft Word as a word-processing software

Microsoft Word is a powerful word-processing software that allows users to create, edit, and format text-based documents. It's a versatile tool widely used for tasks such as writing letters, creating resumes, drafting reports, and much more. For beginners and seniors, understanding the overview of Microsoft Word involves becoming familiar with its key features and functionalities.

Key Components of Microsoft Word:

1. **User Interface:**

    - The Word interface is user-friendly, with a ribbon at the top containing tabs (e.g., Home, Insert, Page Layout) and a document area where you input and format text.

2. **Document Creation:**

    - Users can start a new document or open an existing one. Microsoft Word supports various document types, including letters, reports, resumes, and more.

3. **Text Entry and Editing:**

    - Word allows users to type and edit text seamlessly. Basic operations include typing, deleting, and moving text using the keyboard and mouse.

4. **Formatting Tools:**

    - Formatting tools enable users to change the appearance of text. This includes adjusting font styles, sizes, colors, bold, italic, underline, and more.

5. **Paragraph Formatting:**

- Users can align text (left, center, right, or justified) and set line spacing and paragraph indentation for a polished look.

6. **Lists and Bullets:**
   - Word makes it easy to create bulleted and numbered lists for organized content.

7. **Page Layout:**
   - Page layout features allow users to set margins, adjust page orientation (portrait or landscape), and add headers and footers.

8. **Inserting Elements:**
   - Users can insert various elements into their documents, including images, tables, charts, hyperlinks, and more.

9. **Spell Check and Grammar:**
   - Word includes built-in spell check and grammar tools to help users proofread and correct errors.

10. **Printing:**
    - Printing options enable users to print their documents with various settings, such as page layout, number of copies, and more.

11. **Saving and Opening Documents:**
    - Word allows users to save their documents in different formats and locations. Users can also open existing documents for further editing.

Tips for Beginners and Seniors:

1. **Start with Basic Skills:**
   - Begin with the fundamentals like typing, formatting text, and saving documents.

2. **Use Templates:**

- Explore templates available in Word for various document types. Templates provide a starting point with pre-designed formats.

3. **Explore the Ribbon Tabs:**
   - Familiarize yourself with the Home, Insert, and Page Layout tabs on the ribbon. These tabs contain essential tools for document creation and formatting.

4. **Take Advantage of Help Features:**
   - Word offers helpful features like the Tell Me box, which allows users to search for specific tasks and get step-by-step guidance.

5. **Practice Regularly:**
   - Practice typing, formatting, and using different features regularly to build confidence and proficiency.

Importance in creating documents, letters, and reports.

Understanding the importance of creating documents, letters, and reports using tools like Microsoft Word is crucial for both seniors and beginners.

Importance for Seniors:

1. **Communication:**

- **Letters to Family and Friends:** Seniors can use word-processing software to write letters to family and friends, fostering communication and staying connected with loved ones.

2. **Preserving Memories:**

- **Creating Personal Documents:** Word processors enable seniors to document their life stories, memories, and experiences, preserving them for future generations.

3. **Learning and Hobbies:**

- **Exploring New Interests:** Seniors can use document creation for pursuing hobbies, such as writing poetry, short stories, or recording recipes.

4. Health Records:

- **Recording Health Information:** Word documents provide a platform for seniors to maintain personal health records, including medication schedules, doctor's appointments, and medical history.

5. Community Engagement:

- **Contributing to Community:** Seniors can use document creation for community engagement, such as writing newsletters for local clubs or groups.

Importance for Beginners:

1. Academic and Professional Growth:

- **Creating Reports for School/Work:** Beginners, especially students, can use word processors to create reports, essays, and assignments for academic purposes. Similarly, professionals can draft reports for work.

2. Resume Building:

- **Crafting Resumes and Cover Letters:** Beginners entering the job market can use word processors to create professional resumes and cover letters, showcasing their skills and qualifications.

3. Business Communication:

- **Writing Emails and Business Letters:** Word-processing skills are essential for effective business communication, including drafting emails, formal letters, and other professional correspondence.

4. Organizing Information:

- **Note-Taking and Documentation:** Beginners can use word processors for note-taking and organizing information, enhancing their ability to manage data effectively.

5. Creative Expression:

- **Creative Writing and Expression:** Word processors provide a platform for beginners to explore creative writing, express ideas, and experiment with different writing styles.

6. Digital Literacy:

- **Building Digital Literacy:** Learning word-processing skills is a foundational aspect of digital literacy, a crucial skill in today's technology-driven world.

7. Collaboration:

- **Collaborative Projects:** Beginners can collaborate on projects by sharing and editing documents, fostering teamwork and enhancing their collaborative skills.

Shared Importance:

1. Efficiency and Professionalism:

- **Efficient Communication:** Whether for personal or professional use, creating documents ensures clear, concise, and professional communication.

2. Record Keeping:

- **Maintaining Records:** Both seniors and beginners benefit from using word processors to maintain organized records, whether for personal matters or work-related documentation.

3. Skill Development:

- **Continuous Learning:** Engaging with word-processing software promotes ongoing skill development, helping both groups stay current with technology trends.

Why Use Microsoft Word?

Microsoft Word is a widely used word-processing software that offers numerous advantages for document creation. Here are several key benefits:

1. **User-Friendly Interface:**
   - Word provides an intuitive and user-friendly interface, making it accessible to beginners and those with varying levels of computer literacy.

2. **Versatility:**
   - Word is versatile and can be used to create a wide range of documents, including letters, resumes, reports, newsletters, and more.

3. **Ease of Formatting:**
   - The software offers powerful formatting tools that allow users to customize the appearance of text, paragraphs, and entire documents. This includes font styles, sizes, colors, alignment, and spacing.

4. **Templates:**
   - Word provides pre-designed templates for various document types, saving time and ensuring a professional look. Users can choose templates for resumes, newsletters, brochures, and more.

5. **Spell Check and Grammar:**
   - The built-in spell check and grammar tools help users catch and correct errors, ensuring that documents are free from typos and grammatical mistakes.

6. **Collaboration Features:**
   - Word supports collaborative work by allowing users to share documents and work on them simultaneously. Real-time collaboration features enhance teamwork and streamline the editing process.

7. **Track Changes:**

- The "Track Changes" feature enables users to make edits to a document that can be reviewed, accepted, or rejected by others. This is particularly useful in collaborative and editorial scenarios.

8. **Integration with Other Microsoft Office Apps:**
   - Word seamlessly integrates with other Microsoft Office applications such as Excel and PowerPoint. This allows for easy insertion of tables, charts, and other elements created in these apps.

9. **Automation with Macros:**
   - Advanced users can create and use macros to automate repetitive tasks, saving time and enhancing efficiency.

10. **SmartArt and Graphics:**
    - Word offers tools for creating visual elements like SmartArt graphics, charts, and images, allowing users to enhance the visual appeal of their documents.

11. **Table Functionality:**
    - Word's table functionality enables users to create, edit, and format tables easily, making it a valuable tool for organizing and presenting data.

12. **Document Navigation:**
    - The navigation pane and search features make it easy to navigate through large documents, locate specific content, and manage document structure.

13. **Cross-Platform Compatibility:**
    - Documents created in Word are compatible across different platforms, ensuring that users can access and edit their files on Windows, macOS, and even online through Microsoft 365.

14. **Version History:**

- Word automatically saves versions of documents, allowing users to revert to previous versions if needed. This helps prevent data loss and provides a safety net for document changes.

15. **Security Features:**
    - Word includes features such as password protection and encryption to enhance document security, restricting access to sensitive information.

16. **Cloud Integration:**
    - Microsoft Word seamlessly integrates with cloud services, allowing users to save and access documents from cloud storage platforms like OneDrive, Google Drive, or Dropbox.

Compatibility and integration with other Microsoft Office applications

One of the significant advantages of Microsoft Word is its seamless compatibility and integration with other Microsoft Office applications. This interoperability enhances efficiency and allows users to create comprehensive documents that may involve data from various sources. Here's how Microsoft Word integrates with other Office applications:

1. **Excel Integration:**
    - **Inserting Tables and Data:** Word allows users to embed Excel tables directly into documents. This is useful for incorporating numerical data, calculations, and charts created in Excel.

2. **PowerPoint Integration:**
    - **Embedding Slides:** Users can insert PowerPoint slides into Word documents. This is beneficial when creating reports or documents that require the inclusion of presentation slides.

3. **Outlook Integration:**
    - **Email Integration:** Word is integrated with Outlook, making it easy to draft emails using Word's rich formatting features. Users

can compose emails in Word and send them directly through Outlook.

4. **OneNote Integration:**
   - **Inserting Notes and Content:** Word supports the insertion of content from OneNote, Microsoft's digital note-taking app. This is helpful for incorporating additional information or collaborative notes.

5. **Access Integration:**
   - **Linking to Databases:** For users familiar with Microsoft Access, Word enables the creation of linked databases. This is valuable for incorporating structured data into documents.

6. **Shared User Interface:**
   - **Consistent Ribbon and Tools:** Microsoft Office applications share a similar ribbon interface and menu structure. This consistency simplifies the learning curve for users transitioning between Word, Excel, PowerPoint, and other Office apps.

7. **SmartArt Graphics and Charts:**
   - **Data Visualization:** Users can create SmartArt graphics and charts in Word using data imported from Excel. This ensures consistency in data representation across different Office applications.

8. **Cross-Referencing:**
   - **Linking Between Documents:** Word allows users to create hyperlinks and cross-references to content in other Office documents. This is valuable for maintaining consistency and referencing related information.

9. **Excel Data in Word Tables:**
   - **Linking Excel Data:** Users can link Excel data into Word tables. If the data in the Excel file changes, the linked table in Word can be updated automatically, ensuring data consistency.

10. **Co-Authoring in Real-Time:**
    - **Collaboration Features:** Microsoft Office applications, including Word, support real-time co-authoring. Multiple users can collaborate on a document simultaneously, enhancing teamwork and productivity.

11. **Integration with SharePoint and OneDrive:**
    - **Cloud Services Compatibility:** Word seamlessly integrates with SharePoint and OneDrive for cloud-based collaboration. Documents can be stored, accessed, and edited online, promoting flexibility and accessibility.

12. **Exporting to PDF:**
    - **PDF Creation from Word:** Users can export Word documents to PDF format directly within the Word application. This ensures compatibility with a widely used and standardized document format.

13. **Microsoft Teams Integration:**
    - **Collaboration in Teams:** Word is integrated with Microsoft Teams, a collaboration platform. Users can edit and share Word documents directly within Teams for efficient communication and project management.

Installing Microsoft Word

Installing Microsoft Word is typically part of the Microsoft Office suite installation process. Here's a step-by-step guide for beginners and seniors on how to install Microsoft Word:

For Microsoft 365 Subscription (Online Installation):

Step 1: Check System Requirements

Before you begin, ensure that your computer meets the system requirements for Microsoft 365.

Step 2: Purchase or Verify Microsoft 365 Subscription

- If you don't have a Microsoft 365 subscription, you'll need to purchase one. If you have a subscription, ensure it is active.

Step 3: Sign In to Your Microsoft Account

- Open a web browser and go to the official Microsoft 365 website.
- Sign in with your Microsoft account or create a new account if you don't have one.

Step 4: Choose a Subscription Plan

- Select a Microsoft 365 subscription plan that includes Word. Follow the on-screen instructions to complete the purchase.

Step 5: Access the Microsoft 365 Portal

- Once your subscription is active, go to the Microsoft 365 portal.

Step 6: Install Office Apps

- Find the option to install Office apps and click on it.
- Follow the on-screen instructions to download and install Microsoft Office, including Word.

Step 7: Launch Microsoft Word

- After installation, you can launch Microsoft Word from the Start menu (Windows) or Applications folder (macOS).
- Sign in with your Microsoft account to activate the software.

For Standalone Office Version (DVD or Download):

Step 1: Purchase or Obtain Microsoft Office DVD

- If you have a physical DVD, insert it into your computer's DVD drive. If you're downloading, ensure you have the product key.

Step 2: Run the Setup

- Open File Explorer (Windows) or Finder (macOS) and navigate to the DVD drive or the folder where you downloaded the Office setup file.

Step 3: Begin Installation

- Double-click on the setup file to initiate the installation process.

Step 4: Enter Product Key

- If prompted, enter the product key that came with your Office package.

Step 5: Choose Installation Options

- Follow the on-screen prompts to choose installation options, including which Office apps to install.

Step 6: Complete Installation

- Wait for the installation process to complete. This may take some time.

Step 7: Launch Microsoft Word

- Once installed, you can launch Microsoft Word from the Start menu (Windows) or Applications folder (macOS).
- Activate the software by entering your Microsoft account details.

For Microsoft Office Online:

Step 1: Go to Office Online

- Open a web browser and go to the Office Online website.

Step 2: Sign In or Create Microsoft Account

- Sign in with your Microsoft account or create a new account.

Step 3: Access Word Online

- From the Office Online portal, click on Word.

Step 4: Create or Edit Documents

- Use Word Online directly in your web browser to create, edit, and save documents.

Exploring the Word Interface
Ribbon

Introduction to the Ribbon and its tabs.

The Ribbon is a central element of the Microsoft Office interface, including Microsoft Word. It is designed to provide an intuitive and organized way for users to access various commands and features. Each tab on the Ribbon represents a category of functions related to the task at hand. Here's an introduction to the Ribbon and its tabs:

The Ribbon:

- **Definition:** The Ribbon is a graphical user interface element introduced in Microsoft Office applications, including Word, Excel, and PowerPoint. It replaced the traditional menu and toolbar system with a tabbed toolbar containing groups of related tools and commands.

- **Purpose:** The Ribbon is designed to make it easier for users to find and use the commands they need while working on documents, spreadsheets, or presentations. It organizes features into logical categories to streamline the user experience.

Tabs on the Ribbon:

1. **Home Tab:**

    - **Purpose:** The Home tab is the default tab and contains commonly used commands for formatting text, paragraphs, and overall document layout. It's where you'll find tools for font formatting, styles, clipboard functions, and basic editing.

2. **Insert Tab:**

    - **Purpose:** The Insert tab is used for adding various elements to your document. This includes inserting tables, pictures, shapes, charts, hyperlinks, headers, footers, and more.

3. **Page Layout Tab:**

- **Purpose:** The Page Layout tab focuses on the overall layout and appearance of the document. It includes options for adjusting margins, orientation (portrait or landscape), size, and themes.

4. **References Tab:**

- **Purpose:** The References tab is dedicated to features related to creating and managing citations, references, and table of contents. It includes tools for inserting footnotes, endnotes, and managing bibliographies.

5. **Mailings Tab:**

- **Purpose:** The Mailings tab is primarily used for mail merge functions. It includes tools for creating and managing mail merge documents, envelopes, and labels.

6. **Review Tab:**

- **Purpose:** The Review tab is focused on reviewing and editing documents. It includes tools for spell-checking, tracking changes, adding comments, and protecting documents.

7. **View Tab:**

- **Purpose:** The View tab is for controlling the way you view and navigate your document. It includes options for adjusting document views, showing/hiding rulers and gridlines, and zooming in and out.

Additional Tabs:

- Depending on your version of Word and any additional plugins or features, you may have tabs like "Developer," "Add-ins," or others.

Groups and Commands within Tabs:

- **Groups:** Each tab is further divided into groups, which are collections of related commands. For example, the Font group in the Home tab includes options for formatting text.

- **Commands:** Commands are specific actions or tools within a group. For instance, the Bold and Italic buttons in the Font group are commands for formatting text.

Customization:
- Users can customize the Ribbon by adding or removing tabs, groups, or commands to better suit their preferences and workflow. This flexibility allows users to tailor the interface to their specific needs.

Commonly used tabs like Home, Insert, and Layout.

Home Tab
- **Purpose:**
    - The Home tab is the default tab when you open Microsoft Word. It contains frequently used commands for basic text formatting, paragraph formatting, and document editing.
- **Key Groups and Commands:**

1. **Clipboard Group:**
    - **Cut, Copy, Paste:** Basic clipboard functions for cutting, copying, and pasting text.
    - **Format Painter:** Copies the formatting of selected text to apply elsewhere.

2. **Font Group:**
    - **Font Styles:** Options for changing the font, font size, and font color.
    - **Bold, Italic, Underline:** Formatting options for emphasizing text.

3. **Paragraph Group:**
    - **Alignment:** Options for aligning text (left, center, right, justified).
    - **Bullets and Numbering:** Create bulleted or numbered lists.

4. **Styles Group:**

- **Quick Styles:** Predefined styles for text formatting.
- **Clear Formatting:** Removes formatting from selected text.

5. **Editing Group:**
   - **Find, Replace:** Tools for searching and replacing text.
   - **Select Text:** Options for selecting text efficiently.

Insert Tab

- **Purpose:**
  - The Insert tab is used for adding various elements to your document, including tables, pictures, links, headers, and more.

- **Key Groups and Commands:**

1. **Pages Group:**
   - **Cover Page, Blank Page:** Insert pre-designed cover pages or blank pages.
   - **Page Break:** Start a new page at the cursor position.

2. **Tables Group:**
   - **Table:** Insert a table with a specified number of rows and columns.
   - **Illustrations:** Insert pictures, shapes, and online images.

3. **Illustrations Group:**
   - **Pictures, Online Pictures:** Insert images from your computer or online sources.
   - **Shapes, SmartArt:** Add shapes and SmartArt graphics.

4. **Links Group:**
   - **Hyperlink:** Create hyperlinks to websites, files, or other locations.
   - **Bookmark:** Add bookmarks to specific locations in the document.

5. **Header & Footer Group:**
    - **Header, Footer:** Insert headers and footers to customize the top and bottom of pages.
    - **Page Number:** Add page numbers to the document.

Layout Tab

- **Purpose:**
    - The Layout tab is focused on the overall layout and appearance of the document. It includes options for adjusting margins, orientation, size, and themes.
- **Key Groups and Commands:**

1. **Page Setup Group:**
    - **Margins:** Adjust the margins of the document.
    - **Orientation:** Switch between portrait and landscape modes.

2. **Size Group:**
    - **Size:** Change the paper size of the document.
    - **Columns:** Divide the document into multiple columns.

3. **Themes Group:**
    - **Themes:** Apply pre-designed themes to the entire document.
    - **Colors, Fonts, Effects:** Customize the visual appearance of the document.

4. **Paragraph Group:**
    - **Spacing:** Set line spacing and paragraph spacing.
    - **Indentation:** Adjust left and right indentation.

5. **Arrange Group:**

- **Position, Wrap Text:** Arrange and wrap text around images or objects.
- **Bring Forward, Send Backward:** Change the order of objects.

Backstage View

Accessing Backstage View For Document Management

Backstage View in Microsoft Word is a centralized place where you can manage your documents, perform various file-related tasks, and access document settings. Here's how you can access Backstage View for document management:

Step-by-Step Guide:

1. **Open Microsoft Word:**

   - Launch Microsoft Word on your computer.

2. **Create or Open a Document:**

   - Either create a new document or open an existing one by clicking on "File" in the upper-left corner and selecting "Open" to choose an existing file.

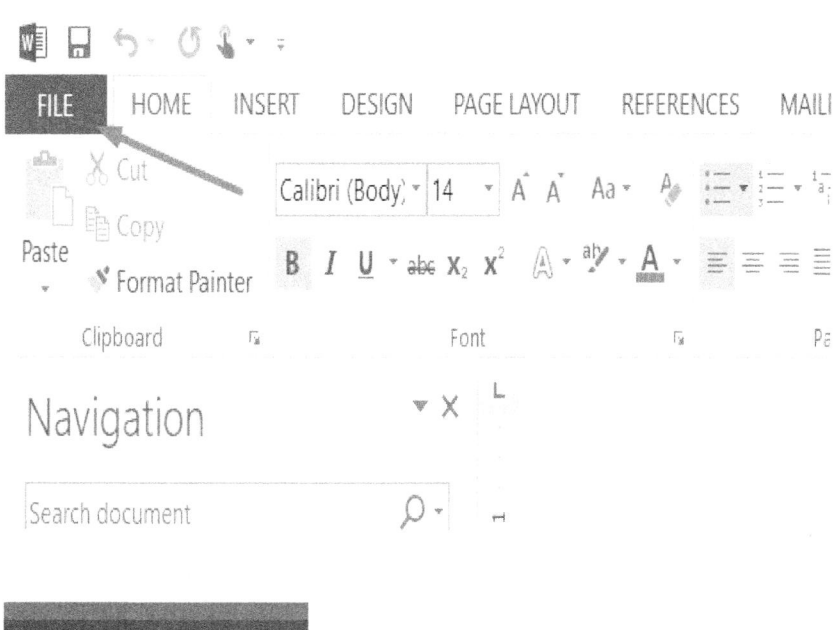

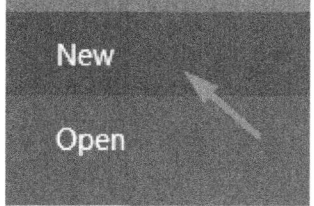

Related Documents

Open File Location

Show All Properties

3. **Access Backstage View:**

    - Once you have a document open or a new one created, click on the "File" tab in the upper-left corner of the screen. This action takes you to Backstage View.

4. **Navigate Backstage View Options:**

    - In Backstage View, you'll find a range of options organized on the left side of the screen. These options may include:

        - **Info:** View document properties, check compatibility, and manage versions.

        - **New:** Create a new document, template, or blog post.

        - **Open:** Open an existing document or browse recent documents.

        - **Save As:** Save the current document with a new name or in a different location.

        - **Print:** Set up and print the document.

        - **Share:** Share the document with others or send it via email.

        - **Export:** Save the document in a different format, such as PDF.

        - **Close:** Close the current document.

5. **Document Information:**
   - On the right side of Backstage View, you may see information about the current document, including the file path, size, and modification date.

6. **Perform Document Management Tasks:**
   - Depending on your needs, you can perform various document management tasks from Backstage View, such as saving, printing, sharing, and exporting.

Additional Tips:

- **Keyboard Shortcut:**
  - You can quickly access Backstage View by using the keyboard shortcut **Alt + F**.

- **Recent Documents:**
  - Backstage View often displays a list of recent documents for quick access.

- **Info Section:**
  - In the "Info" section of Backstage View, you can access document properties, permissions, and version history.

File Options, Saving, And Opening Documents.
File Options, Saving, and Opening Documents:

1. **Open Microsoft Word:**
   - Launch Microsoft Word on your computer.

2. **Create a New Document or Open an Existing One:**
   - You can create a new document by selecting "Blank Document" or open an existing one by clicking on "File" and choosing "Open."

3. **Access Backstage View:**

- Click on the "File" tab in the upper-left corner of the screen to access Backstage View.

4. **File Options and Info:**

    - In Backstage View, you'll see various options on the left side. Click on "Info" to view document properties and additional file-related information.

5. **Save the Document:**

    - To save the document, click on "Save" or "Save As" in Backstage View.

    - If it's a new document, you'll be prompted to choose a location and enter a file name.

    - If it's an existing document, clicking "Save" will overwrite the existing file. Use "Save As" to save a copy with a new name or in a different location.

6. **Open an Existing Document:**

    - To open an existing document, click on "Open" in Backstage View.

    - Navigate to the location where your document is stored, select it, and click "Open."

7. **Recent Documents:**

    - In Backstage View, you'll also see a list of recent documents for quick access. Click on a document in the "Recent" section to open it directly.

8. **Additional Save Options:**

    - Under "Save As," you can choose different formats for saving your document, such as PDF or other Word formats.

    - Use "Export" for additional options like creating a PDF, sending the document as an email attachment, or saving it in other formats.

9. **AutoSave and Versions:**

    - Backstage View also provides information about AutoSave settings and allows you to access version history under the "Manage Versions" section.

10. **Close Backstage View:**

    - To return to the main document view, click anywhere outside of Backstage View or use the "Esc" key.

Quick Access Toolbar
Customizing the Quick Access Toolbar

Customizing the Quick Access Toolbar (QAT) in Microsoft Word allows you to add frequently used commands, making them easily accessible. Here's a step-by-step guide on how to customize the Quick Access Toolbar:

Customizing the Quick Access Toolbar:

1. **Access Backstage View:**

    - Open Microsoft Word and click on the "File" tab in the upper-left corner to access Backstage View.

2. **Go to Options:**

    - In Backstage View, select "Options" at the bottom of the left-hand menu. This opens the Word Options dialog box.

3. **Navigate to Quick Access Toolbar Options:**

    - In the Word Options dialog box, choose the "Quick Access Toolbar" category on the left.

4. **Choose Commands:**

    - In the "Choose commands from" dropdown menu, select the category containing the commands you want to add to the Quick Access Toolbar. Common categories include "Popular Commands" and specific tabs like "Home" or "Insert."

5. **Add Commands to QAT:**
    - Select the command you want to add from the left column, then click the "Add > >" button to move it to the right column. This adds the command to the Quick Access Toolbar.

6. **Adjust Order:**
    - Use the up and down arrows on the right side to adjust the order of commands in the Quick Access Toolbar. The commands are displayed from left to right in the order they appear in this list.

7. **Modify Existing Commands:**
    - You can also customize existing commands on the Quick Access Toolbar. Select a command on the right side, and then use the "Modify" button to change its icon or display name.

8. **Remove Commands:**
    - To remove a command from the Quick Access Toolbar, select it in the right column and click the "Remove" button.

9. **Choose Icon-Only or Text Options:**
    - Use the "Show Quick Access Toolbar below the Ribbon" checkbox to choose whether the toolbar appears above or below the Ribbon.
    - You can also select "Show Quick Access Toolbar above the Ribbon" for a more compact view.

10. **Click "OK" to Apply Changes:**
    - After customizing the Quick Access Toolbar to your liking, click the "OK" button in the Word Options dialog box to apply the changes.

Adding Commands to the Quick Access Toolbar

1. **Access Backstage View:**

    - Open Microsoft Word and click on the "File" tab in the upper-left corner to access Backstage View.

2. **Go to Options:**

    - In Backstage View, select "Options" at the bottom of the left-hand menu. This opens the Word Options dialog box.

3. **Navigate to Quick Access Toolbar Options:**

    - In the Word Options dialog box, choose the "Quick Access Toolbar" category on the left.

4. **Choose Commands:**

    - In the "Choose commands from" dropdown menu, select the category containing the commands you want to add to the Quick Access Toolbar. Common categories include "Popular Commands" and specific tabs like "Home" or "Insert."

5. **Add Commands to QAT:**

    - Select the command you want to add from the left column, then click the "Add > >" button to move it to the right column. This adds the command to the Quick Access Toolbar.

6. **Adjust Order (Optional):**

    - Use the up and down arrows on the right side to adjust the order of commands in the Quick Access Toolbar. The commands are displayed from left to right in the order they appear in this list.

7. **Click "OK" to Apply Changes:**

    - After adding commands, click the "OK" button in the Word Options dialog box to apply the changes.

    -

Removing Commands from the Quick Access Toolbar

1. **Access Backstage View:**

    - If you're not already in Backstage View, click on the "File" tab to access it.

2. **Go to Options:**

    - Select "Options" at the bottom of the left-hand menu to open the Word Options dialog box.

3. **Navigate to Quick Access Toolbar Options:**

    - In the Word Options dialog box, choose the "Quick Access Toolbar" category on the left.

4. **Remove Commands from QAT:**

    - In the right column, which displays the commands currently in the Quick Access Toolbar, select the command you want to remove.
    - Click the "Remove < <" button to take it out of the Quick Access Toolbar.

5. **Click "OK" to Apply Changes:**

    - After removing commands, click the "OK" button in the Word Options dialog box to apply the changes.

Now, your Quick Access Toolbar will reflect the changes, including the newly added commands and the removal of those you no longer need. Customizing the Quick Access Toolbar according to your workflow enhances your efficiency in Microsoft Word.

Navigating a Document

Basics of navigating through a Word document

Navigating through a Word document efficiently is crucial for a smooth workflow. Here are the basics of navigating through a Word document:

Using the Mouse:

1. **Scrolling:**

    - **Vertical Scroll Bar:** Use the vertical scroll bar on the right side of the document to scroll up or down.

    - **Mouse Wheel:** Scroll the mouse wheel forward to move down and backward to move up.

    - **Scroll Arrows:** Click the scroll arrows at the top or bottom of the vertical scroll bar to move one line at a time.

2. **Navigation Pane:**

    - Open the Navigation Pane by clicking on the "View" tab and selecting "Navigation Pane." It allows you to navigate by headings, pages, or search results.

    - You can also use the search bar in the Navigation Pane to find specific text in the document.

3. **Page Thumbnails:**

    - Click the "View" tab and select "Thumbnails" to display page thumbnails on the left side. Click a thumbnail to jump to a specific page.

Using the Keyboard:

1. **Arrow Keys:**

    - Use the arrow keys on the keyboard to move the cursor up, down, left, or right.

2. **Page Up and Page Down:**

    - Press "Page Up" to move up one screen, and "Page Down" to move down one screen.

3. **Ctrl + Arrow Keys:**

   - Hold down the "Ctrl" key while pressing the arrow keys to move the cursor by word rather than by character.

4. **Ctrl + Home and Ctrl + End:**

   - Press "Ctrl + Home" to move the cursor to the beginning of the document.
   - Press "Ctrl + End" to move the cursor to the end of the document.

5. **Ctrl + Page Up and Ctrl + Page Down:**

   - Use "Ctrl + Page Up" to move to the previous page.
   - Use "Ctrl + Page Down" to move to the next page.

Using the Navigation Pane:

1. **Headings:**

   - If your document has headings, use the Navigation Pane to jump to different sections by clicking on the headings.

2. **Pages:**

   - In the Navigation Pane, click "Pages" to see thumbnails of each page and quickly navigate to a specific page.

3. **Search:**

   - Use the Navigation Pane's search function to find specific words or phrases in your document.

Using Go To:

1. **Go To a Page:**

   - Press "Ctrl + G" to open the "Go To" dialog box. Enter the page number and click "Go To."

2. **Go To a Section:**

   - In the "Go To" dialog box, select "Section" to jump to a specific section in your document.

By mastering these basic navigation techniques, you can quickly move around your Word document, making editing and reviewing more efficient.

Using Scroll Bars, Page Navigation, and Keyboard Shortcuts.

Navigating through a Word document involves using scroll bars, page navigation, and keyboard shortcuts. Here's a comprehensive guide on how to utilize these tools:

Scroll Bars:

1. **Vertical Scroll Bar:**
   - Located on the right side of the document window.
   - **To Scroll:**
     - Click and drag the scroll box.
     - Click the up or down arrow at the top or bottom of the scroll bar.
     - Use the mouse wheel (if available).

2. **Horizontal Scroll Bar:**
   - Appears at the bottom of the document window when the document width exceeds the window width.
   - **To Scroll:**
     - Click and drag the scroll box.
     - Click the left or right arrow at the ends of the scroll bar.
     - Use the mouse wheel while holding down the "Shift" key (if available).

Page Navigation:

1. **Page Up and Page Down:**
   - **To Move:**
     - Press "Page Up" to move up one screen.

- Press "Page Down" to move down one screen.

2. **Ctrl + Home and Ctrl + End:**

    - **To Move:**

        - Press "Ctrl + Home" to move to the beginning of the document.
        - Press "Ctrl + End" to move to the end of the document.

3. **Ctrl + Page Up and Ctrl + Page Down:**

    - **To Move:**

        - Press "Ctrl + Page Up" to move to the previous page.
        - Press "Ctrl + Page Down" to move to the next page.

Keyboard Shortcuts:

1. **Arrow Keys:**

    - **To Move:**

        - Use the arrow keys to move the cursor up, down, left, or right.

2. **Ctrl + Arrow Keys:**

    - **To Move by Word:**

        - Hold down the "Ctrl" key while pressing the arrow keys to move the cursor by word.

3. **Ctrl + Backspace and Ctrl + Delete:**

    - **To Delete:**

        - Press "Ctrl + Backspace" to delete the word to the left of the cursor.
        - Press "Ctrl + Delete" to delete the word to the right of the cursor.

4. **Ctrl + Z and Ctrl + Y:**

- **Undo and Redo:**
    - Press "Ctrl + Z" to undo the last action.
    - Press "Ctrl + Y" to redo the last undone action.

5. **Ctrl + F:**

    - **Find:**
        - Press "Ctrl + F" to open the Find dialog box. Enter the text you want to find.

6. **Ctrl + H:**

    - **Find and Replace:**
        - Press "Ctrl + H" to open the Find and Replace dialog box. Enter the text you want to find and replace.

7. **Ctrl + G:**

    - **Go To:**
        - Press "Ctrl + G" to open the Go To dialog box. Enter the page number or section you want to navigate to.

Using the Navigation Pane:

1. **Open Navigation Pane:**
    - Click on the "View" tab and select "Navigation Pane."

2. **Navigate by Headings, Pages, or Results:**
    - In the Navigation Pane, you can click on "Headings" to navigate by heading levels, "Pages" to see page thumbnails, or use the search bar to find specific text.

Document Formatting

Font Styles and Sizes

Formatting text with different fonts, styles, and sizes in Microsoft Word allows you to customize the appearance of your document. Here's a step-by-step guide on how to apply these formatting options:

Changing Fonts:

1. **Select Text:**
   - Highlight the text you want to format with a different font.
2. **Home Tab:**
   - Go to the "Home" tab on the Ribbon.
3. **Font Dropdown:**
   - In the "Font" group, locate the "Font" dropdown menu.
4. **Choose a Font:**
   - Click the dropdown menu and select the desired font from the list.

Applying Font Styles:

1. **Select Text:**
   - Highlight the text you want to format with a different style.
2. **Home Tab:**
   - Go to the "Home" tab on the Ribbon.
3. **Font Styles:**
   - In the "Font" group, you'll find options for bold, italic, underline, and more.
4. **Click the Desired Style:**
   - Click the corresponding icon for the style you want to apply.

Changing Font Size:

1. **Select Text:**

- Highlight the text you want to resize.

2. **Home Tab:**

    - Go to the "Home" tab on the Ribbon.

3. **Font Size Dropdown:**

    - In the "Font" group, locate the "Font Size" dropdown menu.

4. **Choose a Font Size:**

    - Click the dropdown menu and select the desired font size from the list.

Combining Font Formatting:

1. **Select Text:**

    - Highlight the text you want to format.

2. **Apply Font, Style, and Size:**

    - Utilize the Font, Style, and Size options in the "Font" group on the "Home" tab to customize the appearance of the selected text.

Keyboard Shortcuts:

- **Bold:**

    - Use **Ctrl + B** to toggle bold formatting.

- **Italic:**

    - Use **Ctrl + I** to toggle italic formatting.

- **Underline:**

    - Use **Ctrl + U** to toggle underline formatting.

Quick Font Formatting Tips:

- **Clear Formatting:**

    - To remove formatting and revert to the default style, select the text and press **Ctrl + Spacebar**.

- **Format Painter:**

- Use the "Format Painter" button on the Ribbon to copy formatting from one text and apply it to another.

Emphasizing text with bold, italic, and underline.

Emphasizing text using bold, italic, and underline formatting in Microsoft Word is a common and effective way to highlight specific words or phrases. Here's how you can apply these formatting options:

Using the Ribbon:

Bold:

- **Select Text:**
  - Highlight the text you want to emphasize.
- **Home Tab:**
  - Go to the "Home" tab on the Ribbon.
- **Bold Button:**
  - In the "Font" group, click the "Bold" button (B).

Italic:

- **Select Text:**
  - Highlight the text you want to italicize.
- **Home Tab:**
  - Go to the "Home" tab.
- **Italic Button:**
  - In the "Font" group, click the "Italic" button (I).

Underline:

- **Select Text:**
  - Highlight the text you want to underline.
- **Home Tab:**
  - Go to the "Home" tab.
- **Underline Button:**

- In the "Font" group, click the "Underline" button (U).

Combining Formatting:

- **Bold and Italic:**
    - Select the text and press **Ctrl + B** for bold, then **Ctrl + I** for italic.
- **Bold and Underline:**
    - Select the text and press **Ctrl + B** for bold, then **Ctrl + U** for underline.
- **Italic and Underline:**
    - Select the text and press **Ctrl + I** for italic, then **Ctrl + U** for underline.

Clearing Formatting:
- **To remove all formatting:**
    - Select the text and press **Ctrl + Spacebar**.

Quick Tips:

- **Format Painter:**
    - Use the "Format Painter" button on the Ribbon to copy formatting from one text and apply it to another.

Paragraph Alignment and Line Spacing
Aligning text left, center, right, or justified.

Aligning text in Microsoft Word is essential for creating a well-organized and visually appealing document. Here's how you can align text to the left, center, right, or justify it:

Using the Ribbon:

Left Align:

- **Select Text:**
    - Highlight the text you want to left-align.
- **Home Tab:**
    - Go to the "Home" tab on the Ribbon.
- **Align Left Button:**
    - In the "Paragraph" group, click the "Align Left" button (or use the keyboard shortcut **Ctrl + L**).

Center Align:

- **Select Text:**
    - Highlight the text you want to center-align.
- **Home Tab:**
    - Go to the "Home" tab.
- **Center Align Button:**
    - In the "Paragraph" group, click the "Center Align" button (or use the keyboard shortcut **Ctrl + E**).

Right Align:

- **Select Text:**
    - Highlight the text you want to right-align.
- **Home Tab:**
    - Go to the "Home" tab.

- **Right Align Button:**
    - In the "Paragraph" group, click the "Align Right" button (or use the keyboard shortcut **Ctrl + R**).

Justify:

- **Select Text:**
    - Highlight the text you want to justify.
- **Home Tab:**
    - Go to the "Home" tab.
- **Justify Button:**
    - In the "Paragraph" group, click the "Justify" button (or use the keyboard shortcut **Ctrl + J**).

Using the Paragraph Dialog Box:

1. **Select Text:**
    - Highlight the text you want to format.
2. **Dialog Box Launcher:**
    - Click the small arrow in the bottom right corner of the "Paragraph" group to open the "Paragraph" dialog box.
3. **Alignment Options:**
    - In the "Paragraph" dialog box, go to the "Alignment" section.
    - Choose the desired alignment option: Left, Center, Right, or Justified.
    - Click "OK" to apply the changes.

Using Keyboard Shortcuts:

- **Left Align:**
    - Select the text and press **Ctrl + L**.
- **Center Align:**

- Select the text and press **Ctrl + E**.
- **Right Align:**
  - Select the text and press **Ctrl + R**.
- **Justify:**
  - Select the text and press **Ctrl + J**.

Adjusting Line Spacing for Readability

Adjusting line spacing in a document is crucial for enhancing readability. Line spacing determines the amount of vertical space between lines of text. Here's how you can adjust line spacing in Microsoft Word:

Using the Ribbon:

1. **Select Text:**
   - Highlight the text you want to format.
2. **Home Tab:**
   - Go to the "Home" tab on the Ribbon.
3. **Line Spacing Options:**
   - In the "Paragraph" group, find the "Line and Paragraph Spacing" button.
4. **Choose Line Spacing:**
   - Click the button to open the menu.
   - Select one of the predefined options like "1.0," "1.15," "1.5," "2.0," or choose "Line Spacing Options" for more customization.
5. **Custom Line Spacing:**
   - If you choose "Line Spacing Options," a dialog box will open.
   - Adjust the "Line spacing" dropdown menu to your desired spacing, such as "Single," "1.5 lines," or "Double."

- You can also set specific spacing before and after paragraphs if needed.

6. **Click "OK" to Apply:**

    - Click "OK" in the dialog box to apply the changes.

Using Keyboard Shortcuts:

- **Single Line Spacing:**

    - Select the text and press **Ctrl + 1**.

- **1.5 Line Spacing:**

    - Select the text and press **Ctrl + 5**.

- **Double Line Spacing:**

    - Select the text and press **Ctrl + 2**.

Applying Line Spacing to the Whole Document:

1. **Select the Entire Document:**

    - Press **Ctrl + A** to select the entire document.

2. **Apply Line Spacing:**

    - Follow the steps mentioned above to adjust line spacing using the Ribbon or keyboard shortcuts.

Adjusting Line Spacing for a Specific Paragraph:

1. **Select Paragraph:**

    - Place the cursor within the paragraph you want to format.

2. **Apply Line Spacing:**

    - Follow the steps mentioned above to adjust line spacing for the selected paragraph.

Adjusting line spacing, can improve the overall readability of your document. Consider the nature of your document and audience preferences when choosing an appropriate line spacing option.

Lists and Bullets

Creating Bulleted And Numbered Lists

Creating bulleted and numbered lists in Microsoft Word helps organize information and makes it easier for readers to follow. Here's how you can create these lists:

Creating Bulleted Lists:

1. **Place the Cursor:**
   - Click where you want to start your bulleted list.

2. **Home Tab:**
   - Go to the "Home" tab on the Ribbon.

3. **Bullets Button:**
   - In the "Paragraph" group, click the "Bullets" button.

4. **Start Typing or Press Enter:**
   - Start typing your first item and press "Enter" to move to the next line with a bullet.
   - Press "Enter" twice to end the bulleted list.

Customizing Bulleted Lists:

1. **Select Bullets:**
   - Select the bulleted list.

2. **Bullets Dropdown:**
   - Click the dropdown arrow next to the "Bullets" button to choose a different bullet style.

3. **Define New Bullet:**
   - To use a custom symbol or picture as a bullet, select "Define New Bullet..."

4. **Choose Bullet Character:**

- In the "Symbol" dialog box, choose a bullet character or click "Font" to select a different font.
- Click "OK" to apply the changes.

Creating Numbered Lists:

1. **Place the Cursor:**
    - Click where you want to start your numbered list.
2. **Home Tab:**
    - Go to the "Home" tab on the Ribbon.
3. **Numbering Button:**
    - In the "Paragraph" group, click the "Numbering" button.
4. **Start Typing or Press Enter:**
    - Start typing your first item and press "Enter" to move to the next line with a number.
    - Press "Enter" twice to end the numbered list.

Customizing Numbered Lists:

1. **Select Numbers:**
    - Select the numbered list.
2. **Numbering Dropdown:**
    - Click the dropdown arrow next to the "Numbering" button to choose a different numbering style.
3. **Define New Number Format:**
    - To create a custom numbering format, select "Define New Number Format..."
4. **Customize Number Format:**
    - In the "Number Format" dialog box, customize the numbering style, starting number, and other options.

- Click "OK" to apply the changes.

Customizing List Styles.

Customizing list styles in Microsoft Word allows you to create lists with personalized formatting, including specific bullet or numbering styles. Here's how you can customize list styles:

Customizing Bulleted List Styles:

1. **Create a Bulleted List:**
    - Start by creating a bulleted list following the steps mentioned earlier.

2. **Select the Bulleted List:**
    - Select the bulleted list that you want to customize.

3. **Bullets Dropdown:**
    - In the "Home" tab, find the "Bullets" button in the "Paragraph" group.

4. **Define New Bullet:**
    - Click "Define New Bullet..." at the bottom of the dropdown menu.

5. **Choose Bullet Character:**
    - In the "Symbol" dialog box, choose a bullet character or click "Font" to select a different font.
    - Click "OK" to apply the changes.

6. **Modify Bullet Style:**
    - To modify the spacing or other characteristics, click the "Modify..." button in the "Define New Bullet" dialog box.
    - Adjust the settings as needed and click "OK."

Customizing Numbered List Styles:

1. **Create a Numbered List:**

- Start by creating a numbered list following the steps mentioned earlier.

2. **Select the Numbered List:**
   - Select the numbered list that you want to customize.

3. **Numbering Dropdown:**
   - In the "Home" tab, find the "Numbering" button in the "Paragraph" group.

4. **Define New Number Format:**
   - Click "Define New Number Format..." at the bottom of the dropdown menu.

5. **Customize Number Format:**
   - In the "Number Format" dialog box, customize the numbering style, starting number, and other options.
   - Click "OK" to apply the changes.

6. **Modify Number Style:**
   - To modify the spacing or other characteristics, click the "Modify..." button in the "Define New Number Format" dialog box.
   - Adjust the settings as needed and click "OK."

Applying Custom List Style to New Lists:

1. **Right-Click on List:**
   - Right-click on a customized list.

2. **Save Selection to List Gallery:**
   - Select "Save Selection to List Gallery."

3. **Name the Style:**
   - Enter a name for your custom style and click "OK."

4. **Applying Custom Style:**
    - When creating a new list, you can now select your custom style from the "List Library."

Page Setup and Margins

Setting Up Page Orientation (Portrait vs. Landscape)

Setting up page orientation, whether portrait or landscape, in Microsoft Word allows you to control the layout of your document.

Changing Page Orientation:

1. **Select the Section:**
    - Click anywhere in the section of the document where you want to change the page orientation. This could be the entire document or a specific section.

2. **Layout Tab:**
    - Go to the "Layout" or "Page Layout" tab on the Ribbon.

3. **Orientation Button:**
    - In the "Page Setup" or "Page Layout" group, locate the "Orientation" button.

4. **Choose Orientation:**
    - Click on either "Portrait" (vertical) or "Landscape" (horizontal) to select the desired page orientation.

Applying Page Orientation to the Whole Document:

- **For the Entire Document:**
    - If you want to change the page orientation for the entire document, you don't need to select a specific section. Just click anywhere in the document.

Customizing Page Orientation for Sections:

- **For Specific Sections:**
  - If you want different page orientations in different sections, make sure to select the section where you want to apply the change.

Checking Page Orientation:

- **Status Bar:**
  - You can also check the current page orientation on the status bar at the bottom of the Word window.

Additional Tips:

- **Page Breaks:**
  - Keep in mind that changing the orientation in the middle of a document may require adding section breaks. Insert a "Next Page" or "Continuous" section break where you want the change to occur.

- **Header and Footer:**
  - When you change the page orientation, make sure to check and adjust headers and footers as needed.

- **Margins:**
  - Adjust the margins if necessary when changing page orientation, as certain orientations may require different margin settings.

Keyboard Shortcuts:

- **For Portrait Orientation:**
  - Press **Ctrl + Alt + P**.

- **For Landscape Orientation:**
  - Press **Ctrl + Alt + L**.

Adjusting Margins for Printing and Document Layout

Adjusting margins in Microsoft Word is essential for optimizing your document layout, whether you're preparing it for printing or just refining the appearance. Here's how you can adjust margins:

Changing Margins:

1. **Layout Tab:**

    - Go to the "Layout" or "Page Layout" tab on the Ribbon.

2. **Margins Button:**

    - In the "Page Setup" or "Page Layout" group, find the "Margins" button.

3. **Choose Margin Preset:**

    - Click on one of the preset margin options, such as "Normal," "Narrow," "Wide," or "Custom Margins."

Customizing Margins:

1. **Custom Margins:**

    - If you choose "Custom Margins" in the Margins menu, the Page Setup dialog box will appear.

2. **Adjust Margins:**

    - In the Margins tab of the Page Setup dialog box, you can manually adjust the top, bottom, left, and right margins.

3. **Apply to:**

    - You can also specify whether you want to apply the changes to the whole document or just selected sections.

4. **Orientation:**

    - Consider the page orientation (portrait or landscape) when adjusting margins.

5. **Paper Size:**

- Make sure the selected paper size matches your intended print size.

6. **Apply and OK:**
   - Click "OK" to apply the changes.

Checking Margins:

- **Ruler:**
  - You can also check and adjust margins using the horizontal and vertical rulers. Click and drag the margin indicators on the rulers to adjust.

Keyboard Shortcuts:

- **For Page Setup Dialog Box:**
  - Press **Alt + P, S, P**.

Margins for Printing:

- **Print Layout View:**
  - Switch to "Print Layout" view to see how your document will look when printed. This view is helpful for adjusting margins for printing.

- **Page Breaks:**
  - When adjusting margins, be mindful of page breaks. Changing margins may affect the layout and cause content to shift to the next or previous page.

- **Print Preview:**
  - Use the "Print Preview" feature to see a preview of how your document will appear when printed.

Typing and Editing Text

Inserting and Editing Text in A Document

Inserting and editing text in a document is a fundamental task in Microsoft Word. Here's a guide on how to do it:

Inserting Text:

1. **Open Your Document:**
   - Open the document in which you want to insert or edit text.

2. **Place the Cursor:**
   - Click where you want to start typing or editing.

3. **Insert Text:**
   - Start typing to insert new text.

Editing Text:

Basic Text Editing:

1. **Select Text:**
   - Click and drag to select the text you want to edit.

2. **Edit Text:**
   - Start typing to replace the selected text, or use the delete key to remove it.

Advanced Text Editing:

1. **Copy and Paste:**
   - Select the text you want to copy, right-click, choose "Copy" (or use **Ctrl + C**), move the cursor to the insertion point, right-click, and choose "Paste" (or use **Ctrl + V**).

2. **Cut and Paste:**

- Select the text you want to cut, right-click, choose "Cut" (or use **Ctrl + X**), move the cursor to the insertion point, right-click, and choose "Paste" (or use **Ctrl + V**).

3. **Undo and Redo:**

    - If you make a mistake, you can undo the last action by pressing **Ctrl + Z**. To redo an action, press **Ctrl + Y**.

Advanced Text Insertion:

1. **Inserting Blank Lines:**

    - Press "Enter" to move to the next line and create a blank line.

2. **Inserting Page Breaks:**

    - To start a new page, place the cursor where you want the page break, go to the "Layout" tab, and click "Breaks" > "Page."

3. **Inserting Special Characters:**

    - Go to the "Insert" tab and click "Symbol" to insert special characters or symbols.

Formatting Text:

1. **Font Styles:**

    - Use the "Home" tab to change font styles, such as bold, italic, or underline.

2. **Font Size and Color:**

    - Adjust the font size and color using options in the "Home" tab.

3. **Alignment:**

    - Use the "Align Left," "Center," "Align Right," and "Justify" options in the "Home" tab to control text alignment.

4. **Line Spacing:**

    - Adjust line spacing using the "Line and Paragraph Spacing" options.

Basic Text Manipulation Techniques

Basic text manipulation techniques in Microsoft Word involve actions like selecting, copying, cutting, pasting, and formatting text. Here's a guide on performing these basic text manipulations:

Selecting Text:

1. **Click and Drag:**
   - To select text, click at the beginning of the text, hold down the mouse button, and drag to the end of the text.

2. **Double-Click:**
   - Double-click a word to select it.

3. **Triple-Click:**
   - Triple-click within a paragraph to select the entire paragraph.

4. **Ctrl + A:**
   - Press **Ctrl + A** to select the entire document.

Copying and Pasting:

1. **Copying Text:**
   - Select the text you want to copy.
   - Right-click and choose "Copy" or use **Ctrl + C**.

2. **Cutting Text:**
   - Select the text you want to cut.
   - Right-click and choose "Cut" or use **Ctrl + X**.

3. **Pasting Text:**
   - Place the cursor where you want to paste the text.
   - Right-click and choose "Paste" or use **Ctrl + V**.

Undo and Redo:

1. **Undo:**
   - Press **Ctrl + Z** to undo the last action.
2. **Redo:**
   - Press **Ctrl + Y** to redo an action that you've undone.

Formatting Text:

1. **Bold, Italic, Underline:**
   - Use the "B," "I," and "U" buttons in the "Home" tab to apply bold, italic, and underline formatting.
2. **Font Size and Color:**
   - Adjust the font size and color using options in the "Home" tab.
3. **Alignment:**
   - Use the alignment options (left align, center, right align, justify) in the "Home" tab to control text alignment.
4. **Bullet and Numbered Lists:**
   - Use the "Bullets" and "Numbering" buttons in the "Home" tab to create bulleted or numbered lists.

Line and Paragraph Spacing:

1. **Line Spacing:**
   - Adjust line spacing using the "Line and Paragraph Spacing" options in the "Home" tab.
2. **Paragraph Indentation:**
   - Use the "Increase Indent" and "Decrease Indent" buttons to control paragraph indentation.

Find and Replace:

1. **Find Text:**

- Use **Ctrl + F** to open the Find dialog box and search for specific text.

2. **Replace Text:**
    - Use **Ctrl + H** to open the Replace dialog box and replace specific text with another.

Keyboard Shortcuts:

1. **Cut (Ctrl + X):**
    - Cut the selected text.

2. **Copy (Ctrl + C):**
    - Copy the selected text.

3. **Paste (Ctrl + V):**
    - Paste copied or cut text.

4. **Undo (Ctrl + Z):**
    - Undo the last action.

5. **Redo (Ctrl + Y):**
    - Redo an action that you've undone.

6. **Select All (Ctrl + A):**
    - Select the entire document.

Copying, Cutting, and Pasting

Copying and Cutting Text for Duplication or Relocation.

Copying and cutting text are essential actions in Microsoft Word, allowing you to duplicate or relocate content within your document. Here's how you can perform these actions:

Copying Text:

1. **Select Text:**
    - Click and drag to select the text you want to copy.

2. **Copy Command:**
    - Right-click on the selected text and choose "Copy" from the context menu.
    - Alternatively, you can use the keyboard shortcut **Ctrl + C** after selecting the text.

3. **Paste Text:**
    - Move the cursor to the location where you want to paste the copied text.
    - Right-click and choose "Paste" from the context menu, or use the keyboard shortcut **Ctrl + V**.

Cutting Text:

1. **Select Text:**
    - Click and drag to select the text you want to cut.

2. **Cut Command:**
    - Right-click on the selected text and choose "Cut" from the context menu.
    - Alternatively, you can use the keyboard shortcut **Ctrl + X** after selecting the text.

3. **Paste Text:**

- Move the cursor to the location where you want to paste the cut text.
- Right-click and choose "Paste" from the context menu, or use the keyboard shortcut **Ctrl + V**.

Copying and Pasting Across Documents:

- **Copying Between Documents:**
    - Open the document from which you want to copy the text.
    - Select and copy the text as mentioned above.
    - Open the destination document.
    - Move the cursor to the desired location and paste the copied text.

Tips:

- **Copy Formatting:**
    - If you want to copy both the text and its formatting, you can use the "Format Painter" tool. Select the text with the desired formatting, click the "Format Painter" button in the Ribbon, and then click on the destination text.

- **Paste Options:**
    - After pasting, you may see a small icon known as the "Paste Options" button. Clicking on it allows you to choose how the pasted text should be formatted.

- **Undo (Ctrl + Z):**
    - If you make a mistake, use the "Undo" command (**Ctrl + Z**) to revert the last action.

Basic Text Manipulation Techniques

Basic text manipulation techniques in Microsoft Word involve actions like selecting, copying, cutting, pasting, and formatting text. Here's a guide on performing these basic text manipulations:

Selecting Text:

1. **Click and Drag:**
    - To select text, click at the beginning of the text, hold down the mouse button, and drag to the end of the text.

2. **Double-Click:**
    - Double-click a word to select it.

3. **Triple-Click:**
    - Triple-click within a paragraph to select the entire paragraph.

4. **Ctrl + A:**
    - Press **Ctrl + A** to select the entire document.

Copying and Pasting:

1. **Copying Text:**
    - Select the text you want to copy.
    - Right-click and choose "Copy" or use **Ctrl + C**.

2. **Cutting Text:**
    - Select the text you want to cut.
    - Right-click and choose "Cut" or use **Ctrl + X**.

3. **Pasting Text:**
    - Place the cursor where you want to paste the text.
    - Right-click and choose "Paste" or use **Ctrl + V**.

Undo and Redo:

1. **Undo:**

- Press **Ctrl + Z** to undo the last action.

2. **Redo:**

    - Press **Ctrl + Y** to redo an action that you've undone.

Formatting Text:

1. **Bold, Italic, Underline:**

    - Use the "B," "I," and "U" buttons in the "Home" tab to apply bold, italic, and underline formatting.

2. **Font Size and Color:**

    - Adjust the font size and color using options in the "Home" tab.

3. **Alignment:**

    - Use the alignment options (left align, center, right align, justify) in the "Home" tab to control text alignment.

4. **Bullet and Numbered Lists:**

    - Use the "Bullets" and "Numbering" buttons in the "Home" tab to create bulleted or numbered lists.

Line and Paragraph Spacing:

1. **Line Spacing:**

    - Adjust line spacing using the "Line and Paragraph Spacing" options in the "Home" tab.

2. **Paragraph Indentation:**

    - Use the "Increase Indent" and "Decrease Indent" buttons to control paragraph indentation.

Find and Replace:

1. **Find Text:**

    - Use **Ctrl + F** to open the Find dialog box and search for specific text.

2. **Replace Text:**
   - Use **Ctrl + H** to open the Replace dialog box and replace specific text with another.

Keyboard Shortcuts:

1. **Cut (Ctrl + X):**
   - Cut the selected text.

2. **Copy (Ctrl + C):**
   - Copy the selected text.

3. **Paste (Ctrl + V):**
   - Paste copied or cut text.

4. **Undo (Ctrl + Z):**
   - Undo the last action.

5. **Redo (Ctrl + Y):**
   - Redo an action that you've undone.

6. **Select All (Ctrl + A):**
   - Select the entire document.

By mastering these basic text manipulation techniques, you can efficiently navigate and manipulate text in Microsoft Word, enhancing your document creation and editing experience.

Find and Replace

Using the Find and Replace feature to locate and modify text.

The Find and Replace feature in Microsoft Word is a powerful tool that allows you to locate specific text and replace it with new content. Here's a guide on how to use Find and Replace:

Finding Text:

1. **Open Find Dialog:**

    - Press **Ctrl + F** or go to the "Home" tab, click on "Find" in the "Editing" group.

2. **Type Search Text:**

    - In the Find dialog box, enter the text you want to find.

3. **Navigate Through Matches:**

    - Click "Find Next" to locate the first instance of the search text. Repeat to find subsequent occurrences.

    - Click "Find All" to display a list of all occurrences in the "Navigation" pane.

Replacing Text:

1. **Open Replace Dialog:**

    - Press **Ctrl + H** or go to the "Home" tab, click on "Replace" in the "Editing" group.

2. **Type Search and Replace Text:**

    - In the Replace dialog box, enter the text you want to find and the replacement text.

3. **Replace or Replace All:**

    - Click "Find Next" to locate the first instance. You can then choose to "Replace" or "Replace All" instances.

- "Replace" replaces one occurrence at a time, and "Replace All" replaces all occurrences in the document.

Advanced Options:

1. **Use Wildcards:**
   - Check the "Use wildcards" option for advanced search patterns.

2. **Match Case:**
   - Check "Match case" to find text with the same uppercase and lowercase letters.

3. **Match Whole Words:**
   - Check "Match whole words only" to find only whole words, not partial matches.

4. **Replace Formatting:**
   - Click "More" in the Replace dialog to access additional options, including the ability to replace formatting.

Tips:

- **Undo (Ctrl + Z):**
  - If you make a mistake during the Find and Replace process, use the "Undo" command (**Ctrl + Z**) to revert the last action.

- **Find Next and Replace (Alt + M):**
  - After clicking "Find Next," you can press **Alt + M** to replace the found instance without clicking the "Replace" button.

Spell Check and Grammar

Utilizing the Built-In Spelling and Grammar Check

Microsoft Word comes equipped with a built-in spelling and grammar check feature to help you catch and correct errors in your documents. Here's a step-by-step guide on how to utilize this feature:

Spelling and Grammar Check:

1. **Open the Document:**
    - Open the Word document that you want to check for spelling and grammar errors.

2. **Review Ribbon:**
    - Go to the "Review" tab on the Ribbon.

3. **Spelling & Grammar Check:**
    - In the "Proofing" group, click on "Spelling & Grammar."

4. **Spelling Errors:**
    - The spelling and grammar check will begin. Word will automatically check for spelling errors first.
    - If a spelling error is found, Word will suggest corrections. You can choose to ignore the suggestion, change the word, or add it to the dictionary.

5. **Grammar Errors:**
    - After checking spelling, Word will proceed to check for grammar errors.
    - Similar to spelling errors, you can review grammar suggestions and choose to accept or ignore them.

6. **Review Pane:**
    - The "Review" pane on the right side of the screen will display the errors and suggestions. You can click on each item to navigate through them.

AutoCorrect and Suggestions:

1. **AutoCorrect Feature:**
   - Word's AutoCorrect feature can automatically fix common spelling and typing errors as you type.

2. **Contextual Suggestions:**
   - Word provides contextual suggestions based on the context of your sentence. Right-click on a word with a red underline to see suggestions.

Customizing Proofing Options:

1. **Proofing Options:**
   - To customize spelling and grammar check settings, click on "Options" at the bottom of the Spelling & Grammar pane.

2. **Set Language Preferences:**
   - In the Proofing Options dialog box, you can set language preferences, customize AutoCorrect options, and more.

Tips:

- **Ignore All or Add to Dictionary:**
  - If you have a term or word that is consistently marked as an error but is correct in your context, you can choose to "Ignore All" or "Add to Dictionary" to prevent Word from flagging it.

- **Review Pane Navigation:**
  - Use the Review pane to quickly navigate through errors and suggestions. Clicking on an item in the pane will take you to that part of the document.

Correcting and Proofreading Documents

Correcting and proofreading documents is a crucial step to ensure accuracy, clarity, and professionalism. Here's a comprehensive guide on how to correct and proofread documents effectively using Microsoft Word:

Correcting Spelling and Grammar Errors:

1. **Run Spelling and Grammar Check:**
    - Go to the "Review" tab.
    - Click on "Spelling & Grammar" in the "Proofing" group.
    - Address suggestions and corrections provided by Word.

2. **AutoCorrect:**
    - Leverage Word's AutoCorrect feature to automatically fix common spelling and typing errors as you type.

3. **Contextual Suggestions:**
    - Right-click on a word with a red underline to see contextual suggestions and corrections.

Correcting Formatting Issues:

1. **Formatting Consistency:**
    - Ensure consistent formatting throughout the document. Check font styles, sizes, and spacing.

2. **Paragraph Alignment:**
    - Confirm that paragraph alignment is consistent. Adjust using the alignment options in the "Home" tab.

3. **Bullet and Numbered Lists:**
    - Check bullet and numbered lists for consistent formatting.

Proofreading for Clarity and Coherence:

1. **Read Aloud:**

- Read the document aloud to identify awkward phrasing, grammatical issues, and improve overall flow.

2. **Consistent Tone and Style:**
    - Ensure a consistent tone and writing style throughout the document.

3. **Sentence Structure:**
    - Check sentence structure for clarity and coherence. Avoid overly complex or convoluted sentences.

4. **Paragraph Transitions:**
    - Verify that paragraphs transition smoothly from one to the next.

5. **Use of Headings:**
    - Confirm that headings and subheadings are used appropriately and consistently.

Reviewing Content:

1. **Factual Accuracy:**
    - Verify the factual accuracy of information presented in the document.

2. **Citations and References:**
    - Check citations and references for accuracy and proper formatting.

3. **Table of Contents:**
    - If applicable, ensure that the table of contents accurately reflects the document's structure.

Utilizing Proofing Tools:

1. **Thesaurus:**
    - Use the built-in Thesaurus to find synonyms and improve word choice.

2. **Translate:**
   - If working with multilingual content, use the Translate feature to check translations.

Reviewing Track Changes (If Collaborating):

1. **Track Changes:**
   - If collaborating with others, use the "Track Changes" feature to review and accept/reject edits.

2. **Comments:**
   - Check and respond to comments left by collaborators.

Tips:

- **Take Breaks:**
  - Take breaks between writing and proofreading sessions to maintain focus.

- **Print for Review:**
  - Print a hard copy for final proofreading. Errors are often easier to spot on paper.

- **Reverse Reading:**
  - Read the document in reverse order to focus on individual sentences without the context of the overall narrative.

- **Use a Style Guide:**
  - Refer to a style guide (e.g., APA, MLA) for specific formatting and citation rules.

- **Get Feedback:**
  - If possible, have a colleague or friend review the document for a fresh perspective.

Chapter 9

Microsoft Excel

Getting Started with Excel

Welcome to the world of Microsoft Excel—a powerful and versatile spreadsheet software that can simplify your data management and analysis tasks. Whether you're a senior seeking to enhance your computer skills or a beginner taking the first steps into the realm of spreadsheets, this introduction aims to provide a friendly and accessible guide to Microsoft Excel.

What is Microsoft Excel?

Microsoft Excel is a spreadsheet program that allows you to organize, analyze, and present data in a structured and visually appealing manner. It's widely used for various purposes, from creating simple lists to managing complex financial data, making it an invaluable tool for both personal and professional tasks.

Why Learn Excel?

Learning Excel offers a multitude of benefits, including:

- **Data Organization:** Excel helps you organize information neatly into rows and columns, making it easy to understand and manage.

- **Calculations and Formulas:** With Excel, you can perform calculations effortlessly using built-in functions and formulas, eliminating the need for manual calculations.

- **Data Analysis:** Excel provides tools for data analysis, including charts and graphs, allowing you to visually interpret your data.

- **Budgeting and Finance:** Manage your finances, create budgets, and track expenses with ease using Excel's financial functions.

- **Increased Productivity:** Excel streamlines repetitive tasks, saving you time and effort in various activities.

Overview of Spreadsheet Software

Spreadsheet software is a powerful tool that has revolutionized the way individuals and businesses manage, analyze, and visualize data. These applications provide a structured grid of rows and columns, turning a simple table into a dynamic workspace capable of performing complex calculations and data manipulation. One of the most widely used and popular spreadsheet software is Microsoft Excel, but various alternatives exist, each offering unique features and capabilities.

Key Characteristics of Spreadsheet Software:

1. **Grid Structure:**
   - Spreadsheets are built on a grid structure, where data is organized into rows and columns, forming individual cells. This structure allows for a systematic arrangement of information.

2. **Data Entry and Storage:**
   - Users can enter and store different types of data in cells, ranging from text and numbers to dates and formulas. The flexibility of data entry makes spreadsheets versatile for various applications.

3. **Formulas and Functions:**
   - Spreadsheets support formulas and functions that enable users to perform calculations and automate processes. Formulas can range from simple arithmetic operations to complex statistical analyses.

4. **Cell Referencing:**
   - Cell referencing allows users to create relationships between different cells. Changes in one cell can automatically update dependent cells, providing a dynamic and interconnected environment.

5. **Data Analysis and Visualization:**
   - Spreadsheet software offers tools for data analysis and visualization. Users can create charts, graphs, and pivot tables to

represent data in a comprehensible and visually appealing manner.

6. **What-If Analysis:**
   - Spreadsheets facilitate "What-If" analysis, allowing users to explore different scenarios by changing input values and observing the impact on calculated results.

7. **Data Sorting and Filtering:**
   - Sorting and filtering functions help organize and analyze data efficiently. Users can rearrange data based on specific criteria or display only relevant information.

8. **Collaboration and Sharing:**
   - Modern spreadsheet software often includes collaboration features, enabling multiple users to work on a document simultaneously. Sharing options facilitate real-time collaboration and version control.

9. **Import and Export Data:**
   - Users can import data from external sources or export data to other formats. This interoperability ensures seamless integration with various applications and databases.

Microsoft Excel: A Leading Spreadsheet Software

Microsoft Excel, part of the Microsoft Office suite, stands as one of the most widely adopted spreadsheet applications. Known for its user-friendly interface and robust functionality, Excel has become a staple for individuals, businesses, and organizations globally.

Installation and Setup

Installing Microsoft Excel

Installing Microsoft Excel is part of the Microsoft Office suite, which includes a range of productivity applications. Here's a step-by-step guide to help you install Microsoft Excel:

Installing Microsoft Office:

1. **Purchase Microsoft Office:**
   - If you haven't already, purchase a valid Microsoft Office license. You can buy it online from the official Microsoft website or authorized retailers.

2. **Acquire Product Key:**
   - Once you purchase Microsoft Office, you will receive a product key. Keep this key handy as you'll need it during the installation process.

Installation Steps:

3. **Download Microsoft Office Installer:**
   - Visit the official Microsoft Office website.
   - Log in with your Microsoft account.

4. **Enter Product Key:**
   - After logging in, enter the product key you received during the purchase process.

5. **Choose Office Version:**
   - Select the version of Microsoft Office you want to install (e.g., Microsoft 365).

6. **Download and Run Installer:**
   - Click on the "Install" button to download the Office installer.
   - Run the downloaded installer to begin the installation process.

7. **Follow Installation Wizard:**
    - The installation wizard will guide you through the process. Follow the on-screen instructions.
    - You may be asked to customize the installation options based on your preferences.

8. **Wait for Installation to Complete:**
    - The installation process may take some time. Wait for it to complete.

9. **Launch Microsoft Excel:**
    - Once the installation is finished, you can launch Microsoft Excel from the Start menu or the desktop shortcut.

10. **Activate Microsoft Office:**
    - Open Excel and sign in with your Microsoft account if prompted. Follow any additional steps to activate your Microsoft Office license.

System Requirements:

Before starting the installation, ensure that your computer meets the system requirements for the version of Microsoft Office you are installing.

- **Internet Connection:** A reliable internet connection is required for downloading the installer and activating Microsoft Office.
- **Storage Space:** Ensure that you have sufficient storage space on your computer for the installation.
- **Operating System:** Microsoft Office is compatible with Windows and macOS. Make sure your operating system is supported.

Configuring Excel Preferences

Configuring Excel preferences allows you to personalize the application to better suit your needs and working style. Here's a guide on how to configure Excel preferences:

Configuring Excel Preferences:

1. **Open Microsoft Excel:**

    - Launch Microsoft Excel on your computer.

2. **Navigate to the "File" Tab:**

    - Click on the "File" tab located in the top-left corner of the Excel window.

3. **Access Excel Options:**

    - Within the File tab, select "Options" at the bottom. This will open the Excel Options dialog box.

General Preferences:

4. **Customize the Ribbon:**

    - In the Excel Options dialog box, select "Customize Ribbon" on the left. Here, you can customize the tabs and groups displayed on the Ribbon.

5. **Change the Office Theme:**

    - Under the "General" category, you can choose a different Office Theme, such as colorful, dark gray, or black, depending on your preference.

Formulas and Calculation Preferences:

6. **Adjust Formula Options:**

    - Navigate to the "Formulas" category on the left. Here, you can customize options related to formula calculation, error checking, and cell references.

Proofing and AutoCorrect Preferences:

7. **Set Proofing Options:**
   - Access the "Proofing" category to configure spelling and grammar check options. You can customize autocorrect settings and language preferences here.

Save and Advanced Preferences:

8. **Specify Save Options:**
   - Under the "Save" category, you can set default save locations, file formats, and AutoRecover options.

9. **Explore Advanced Options:**
   - In the "Advanced" category, you can fine-tune various settings related to editing, display, and working with Excel.

Customize Quick Access Toolbar and Keyboard Shortcuts:

10. **Customize Quick Access Toolbar:**
    - In the Excel Options dialog box, choose "Quick Access Toolbar." Here, you can add or remove commands for quick access.

11. **Modify Keyboard Shortcuts:**
    - Explore the "Customize Ribbon" section to access "Keyboard Shortcuts" where you can customize or modify existing keyboard shortcuts.

User Interface Preferences:

12. **Adjust Display Options:**
    - Back in the Excel Options dialog box, under the "Advanced" category, you can adjust display options, such as the number of sheets in a new workbook and how Excel handles multi-threaded calculations.

Apply Changes:

13. **Apply Changes and Close:**

- After configuring your preferences, click "OK" to apply the changes. Your Excel preferences are now customized according to your settings.

The Excel Interface

Ribbon and Tabs

The Ribbon is a central component of the Microsoft Excel interface, providing a visually organized set of commands and tools to help you navigate and use the software efficiently. It is divided into tabs, each containing groups of related commands. Understanding the Ribbon and tabs is essential for effectively working with Excel. Let's explore this feature:

1. Ribbon Overview:

- The Ribbon is located near the top of the Excel window and is designed to be task-oriented, making it easier to find and use the commands you need.

2. Tabs:

- Tabs are the main categories in the Ribbon, grouping related commands together. Each tab is dedicated to a specific set of tasks or functions.

Common Tabs in Excel:

a. **Home:**

- The "Home" tab is the default tab and contains frequently used commands for formatting, styling, and basic data manipulation.

b. **Insert:**

- The "Insert" tab is used for adding elements to your worksheet, such as charts, tables, pictures, and more.

c. **Page Layout:**

- The "Page Layout" tab is where you can adjust settings related to the appearance of your printed worksheet, including themes, margins, and page orientation.

d. **Formulas:**

- The "Formulas" tab is dedicated to functions and formulas. Here, you can find a wide range of mathematical and logical functions.

e. **Data:**
- The "Data" tab contains tools for working with external data, sorting and filtering, and managing data connections.

f. **Review:**
- The "Review" tab includes tools for proofing, spell-checking, and collaborating with others, such as adding comments and tracking changes.

g. **View:**
- The "View" tab allows you to control the way your workbook is displayed, with options for zooming, arranging windows, and switching between different views.

3. **Groups:**
- Each tab is further divided into groups, which are clusters of related commands. For example, the "Font" group in the "Home" tab contains commands related to text formatting.

4. **Contextual Tabs:**
- Contextual tabs appear on the Ribbon only when you perform certain tasks. For instance, when you select a chart, the "Chart Tools" tab appears with specific chart-related commands.

Cells, Rows, and Columns

Microsoft Excel organizes data into a grid of cells, with each cell identified by a unique combination of a column letter and a row number. Understanding how to work with cells, rows, and columns is fundamental to creating and managing data in Excel. Here's a step-by-step guide:

1. Understanding the Excel Grid:

- Excel's grid is composed of columns labeled with letters (A, B, C, ...) and rows labeled with numbers (1, 2, 3, ...). The intersection of a column and a row is called a cell.

2. Selecting Cells:

- Click on a cell to select it. You can select a single cell, a range of cells, or an entire column or row by clicking and dragging.

3. Inserting Data:

- Double-click on a cell to enter data. You can also type directly into the formula bar at the top of the Excel window.

4. Editing Cells:

- To edit a cell, either double-click on it or select the cell and start typing. Press "Enter" to confirm changes.

5. Moving Around the Worksheet:

- Use the arrow keys on your keyboard to move from cell to cell. Alternatively, use the scroll bars to navigate vertically and horizontally.

6. Inserting Rows and Columns:

- Right-click on the row or column header where you want to insert a new row or column. Choose "Insert" from the context menu.

7. Deleting Rows and Columns:

- Similarly, right-click on the row or column header you want to delete and choose "Delete" from the context menu.

8. Formatting Cells:

- Select the cells you want to format, right-click, and choose "Format Cells." Here, you can adjust the font, number format, alignment, and more.

9. Merging and Unmerging Cells:

- Select the cells you want to merge, right-click, and choose "Merge & Center" from the context menu. To unmerge cells, select the merged cell and click "Unmerge" from the Ribbon.

10. Adjusting Column Width and Row Height:

- Hover your mouse between two column or row headers until the cursor changes. Drag to adjust the width or height.

11. Copying and Pasting:

- Copy cells by selecting them, right-clicking, and choosing "Copy" or using the keyboard shortcut (Ctrl+C). Paste in a new location using "Paste" or (Ctrl+V).

12. Using Formulas:

- Type a formula directly into a cell, starting with an equal sign (e.g., =A1+B1). Press "Enter" to calculate the result.

13. AutoFill Feature:

- Drag the small square at the bottom-right corner of a selected cell to fill adjacent cells with a series or pattern.

14. Sorting Data:

- Select the column you want to sort, go to the "Data" tab, and choose "Sort." Follow the prompts to arrange data in ascending or descending order.

15. Filtering Data:

- Select your data, go to the "Data" tab, and choose "Filter." Use the filter arrows in the column headers to filter and sort data.

Worksheets and Workbooks

Worksheets and workbooks are essential elements in Microsoft Excel, allowing you to organize and manage data efficiently. Here's a step-by-step guide on how to use worksheets and workbooks:

Worksheets:

1. **Understanding Worksheets:**
   - Worksheets are individual tabs within an Excel file (workbook). They are used to organize and manipulate data separately.

2. **Adding a New Worksheet:**
   - To add a new worksheet, click the "+" button at the bottom-left corner of the Excel window. Alternatively, right-click on an existing worksheet tab and select "Insert" > "Worksheet."

3. **Renaming Worksheets:**
   - Double-click on the worksheet tab to rename it. Enter a new name and press "Enter" to confirm.

4. **Navigating Between Worksheets:**
   - Click on different worksheet tabs to switch between them. You can also use keyboard shortcuts (Ctrl + Page Up/Page Down) to move left or right across worksheets.

5. **Copying or Moving Worksheets:**
   - Right-click on a worksheet tab and choose "Move or Copy." Select the destination workbook and position for the worksheet and click "OK" to copy or move the sheet.

6. **Deleting Worksheets:**
   - Right-click on the worksheet tab and select "Delete." Confirm the deletion in the prompt that appears.

Workbooks:

1. **Understanding Workbooks:**

- Workbooks are Excel files that contain one or multiple worksheets. Each workbook opens in a separate window.

2. **Creating a New Workbook:**
   - To create a new workbook, go to the "File" tab, select "New," and then choose "Blank workbook."

3. **Opening an Existing Workbook:**
   - Click on "File" > "Open," navigate to the location of your workbook, select it, and click "Open." Alternatively, double-click the workbook file in File Explorer.

4. **Saving a Workbook:**
   - To save a new workbook, click on "File" > "Save As." Choose a location, enter a name, and select the desired file format. For an existing workbook, click "Save" or "Save As" to overwrite or save a copy.

5. **Closing a Workbook:**
   - Click on "File" > "Close" to close the current workbook. Alternatively, click the "X" button on the workbook window.

6. **Viewing Multiple Workbooks:**
   - To view multiple workbooks side by side, open each workbook, go to the "View" tab, and click on "View Side by Side."

7. **Copying Worksheets Between Workbooks:**
   - Open both workbooks. Right-click the worksheet tab you want to copy, drag it to the other workbook, and release the mouse. Choose "Copy Here."

8. **Linking Data Between Workbooks:**
   - To link data between workbooks, enter a formula in a cell of one workbook referencing cells in another workbook using the format '[WorkbookName]SheetName!CellReference.'

Entering and Formatting Data

Entering data into cells in Microsoft Excel is a fundamental task that forms the basis of creating a spreadsheet. Here's a step-by-step guide on how to enter data into cells:

1. Open Microsoft Excel:

- Launch Microsoft Excel on your computer.

2. Open an Existing Workbook or Create a New One:

- Either open an existing workbook by clicking on "File" > "Open" and selecting the file, or create a new workbook by clicking on "File" > "New" > "Blank Workbook."

3. Navigate to the Desired Worksheet:

- If you have multiple worksheets in your workbook, click on the tab of the worksheet where you want to enter data.

4. Select the Cell:

- Click on the cell where you want to enter data. The selected cell will be outlined, and the cell reference will be displayed in the Name Box (located next to the formula bar).

5. Type the Data:

- Once the cell is selected, start typing the data. You can enter text, numbers, dates, or any other information relevant to your spreadsheet.

6. Press Enter or Tab:

- After typing the data, press "Enter" to move to the cell below or press "Tab" to move to the cell on the right. The entered data will be displayed in the cell.

7. Navigating Cells:

- Use the arrow keys on your keyboard to navigate to adjacent cells. Press "Enter" or "Tab" to move down or to the right. Press "Shift + Enter" to move up, and press "Shift + Tab" to move to the left.

8. Entering Data in a Range:

- To enter data in a range of cells, click and drag to select multiple cells before typing. After entering data in the first cell, press "Enter," and the data will be copied to all selected cells.

9. Editing Data:

- To edit data in a cell, double-click on the cell or press "F2" to enter edit mode. Make the necessary changes and press "Enter" to confirm.

10. Copying and Pasting Data:

- Copy data from one cell (Ctrl + C), select the destination cell, and paste (Ctrl + V). Alternatively, use the "Cut" (Ctrl + X) and "Paste" (Ctrl + V) commands.

11. AutoFill Feature:

- Drag the small square at the bottom-right corner of a selected cell to fill adjacent cells with a series or pattern.

12. Data Validation:

- You can set up data validation to control what type of data is entered into a cell. This is useful for maintaining data accuracy and consistency.

Basic Formatting Options

Basic formatting options in Microsoft Excel allow you to enhance the appearance of your spreadsheet, making it more readable and visually appealing. Here's a step-by-step guide on some fundamental formatting options:

Font Formatting:

1. **Bold, Italics, and Underline:**
    - Select the cell or text you want to format.
    - Use the toolbar or the following keyboard shortcuts:
        - Bold: **Ctrl + B**

- Italics: **Ctrl + I**
- Underline: **Ctrl + U**

2. **Font Color:**
   - Select the cell or text.
   - Use the "Font Color" button in the toolbar or the "Font Color" option in the Home tab.

Cell Formatting:

3. **Cell Fill Color:**
   - Select the cell or range.
   - Use the "Fill Color" button in the toolbar or the "Fill Color" option in the Home tab.

4. **Borders:**
   - Select the cell or range.
   - Use the "Borders" button in the toolbar or the "Borders" option in the Home tab to add or remove cell borders.

Number Formatting:

5. **Number Formats:**
   - Select the cell or range.
   - Use the "Number Format" dropdown in the toolbar or the "Number" group in the Home tab to choose a format (e.g., currency, percentage).

Alignment and Text Control:

6. **Text Alignment:**
   - Select the cell or range.

- Use the alignment options in the toolbar or the alignment group in the Home tab to adjust text alignment (left, center, right) and orientation.

7. **Text Wrap:**
   - Select the cell or range.
   - Use the "Wrap Text" button in the toolbar or the "Wrap Text" option in the Home tab to control text wrapping within a cell.

Column and Row Formatting:

8. **Column Width and Row Height:**
   - Select the column or row by clicking the header.
   - Right-click and choose "Column Width" or "Row Height" to adjust the dimensions.

Conditional Formatting:

9. **Highlight Cells Rules:**
   - Select the cells you want to format.
   - Go to the "Home" tab, click on "Conditional Formatting," and choose "Highlight Cells Rules" to apply formatting based on conditions like values or dates.

10. **Data Bars and Color Scales:**
    - Use "Conditional Formatting" to apply data bars or color scales to highlight values within a range.

AutoFill Feature

The AutoFill feature in Microsoft Excel is a powerful tool that allows you to quickly fill cells with a series or pattern. Whether you're working with numbers, dates, or text, AutoFill can save you time by automatically extending your data based on the existing pattern. Here's how to use the AutoFill feature:

Basic AutoFill:

1. **Enter Data:**

   - Type the starting value in a cell. For example, enter "January" or "1" as the starting point for a series.

2. **Select the Cell Handle:**

   - Move your cursor to the bottom-right corner of the selected cell. A small square, known as the fill handle, will appear.

3. **Drag the Fill Handle:**

   - Click and drag the fill handle down or to the right, depending on the direction you want to fill. Release the mouse button.

4. **Complete the Series:**

   - Excel will automatically fill the cells based on the pattern established by the initial entry.

AutoFill Options:

5. **AutoFill Options Button:**

   - After using AutoFill, a small square with options will appear. Click on it to access AutoFill options.

6. **Copy Cells:**

   - Choose "Copy Cells" to copy the values without formatting or formulas.

7. **Fill Series:**

   - Select "Fill Series" to extend a numerical or date series.

8. **Fill Formatting Only:**

   - Choose "Fill Formatting Only" to copy formatting without changing the values.

9. **Fill Without Formatting:**

- Opt for "Fill Without Formatting" to copy values without formatting.

AutoFill with Custom Lists:

10. **Create a Custom List:**
    - You can create a custom list by going to "File" > "Options" > "Advanced" > "Edit Custom Lists." This is useful for AutoFilling specific sequences.

11. **AutoFill Using Custom List:**
    - Enter the first item from your custom list and use the fill handle to extend the sequence.

AutoFill Handle Double-Click:

12. **Double-Click on Fill Handle:**
    - Double-clicking the fill handle can automatically fill a column or row based on adjacent data.

Formulas and Functions

Understanding formulas is crucial for effective data manipulation and analysis in Microsoft Excel. Formulas are expressions that perform calculations, manipulate data, and return results. They use cell references, operators, functions, and constants. Here's a comprehensive guide to understanding formulas in Excel:

Basics of Excel Formulas:

Formula Structure:

- A formula in Excel starts with an equal sign (=), followed by the expression or function.

Example: **=A1+B1**

Operators:

- Operators perform mathematical or logical operations.
    - Arithmetic Operators: **+** (addition), **-** (subtraction), ***** (multiplication), **/** (division), **%** (percentage).
    - Comparison Operators: **=, <, >, <=, >=, <>** (not equal).

Example: **=C1*0.1**

Cell References:

- Refer to cells in formulas using column and row references.
    - Absolute Reference: **$A$1** (fixed reference)
    - Relative Reference: **A1** (adjusts when copied)

Example: **=$A$1*B1**

Common Excel Functions:

SUM Function:

- Adds up a range of numbers.
    - Example: **=SUM(A1:A10)**

AVERAGE Function:

- Calculates the average of a range of numbers.

- Example: **=AVERAGE(B1:B5)**

IF Function:
- Performs a conditional test and returns different values based on the condition.
    - Example: **=IF(C1>10, "Yes", "No")**

VLOOKUP Function:
- Searches for a value in the first column of a range and returns a corresponding value from another column.
    - Example: **=VLOOKUP(D1, E1:F10, 2, FALSE)**

COUNT Function:
- Counts the number of cells in a range that contain numbers.
    - Example: **=COUNT(G1:G100)**

CONCATENATE Function:
- Combines two or more text strings into one string.
    - Example: **=CONCATENATE(A1, " ", B1)**

NOW Function:
- Returns the current date and time.
    - Example: **=NOW()**

Formula Auditing Tools:

11. **Trace Precedents:**
    - Shows which cells are referred to in the selected cell.
        - Example: Select a cell, go to the "Formulas" tab, and click "Trace Precedents."

12. **Trace Dependents:**
    - Shows which cells depend on the selected cell.
        - Example: Select a cell, go to the "Formulas" tab, and click "Trace Dependents."

13. **Evaluate Formula:**
    - Steps through the evaluation of a formula, showing intermediate results.
        - Example: Select a cell, go to the "Formulas" tab, and click "Evaluate Formula."

Error Checking:

14. **Error Types:**
    - Common errors include **#DIV/0!** (division by zero), **#VALUE!** (wrong data type), and **#REF!** (invalid cell reference).

15. **Error Checking Functions:**
    - **IFERROR**: Handles errors by specifying a value or formula to display in case of an error.
        - Example: **=IFERROR(A1/B1, "Division Error")**

16. **Error Checking Options:**
    - Excel provides options to enable or disable error checking and customize error alert messages.

Formula Tips:

17. **Use Parentheses:**
    - Use parentheses to control the order of operations in complex formulas.
        - Example: **=(A1+B1)*C1**

18. **AutoSum Feature:**
    - Click the "AutoSum" button to quickly insert a SUM formula.
        - Example: Select a cell, click "AutoSum" in the toolbar.

19. **Function Arguments:**
    - Understand the arguments required for each function. Excel provides hints and descriptions for each argument.

20. **Formula Examples:**
    - Practice creating formulas for common tasks, such as calculating percentages, averages, and totals.

Performing Basic Arithmetic Operations

Performing basic arithmetic operations in Microsoft Excel involves using mathematical operators within formulas. Here's a guide on how to perform addition, subtraction, multiplication, and division:

Addition:

To add numbers in Excel, you can use the **+** operator.

1. **Example:**
    - Type the following formula in a cell: **=A1 + B1**
    - Press "Enter" to get the sum of the numbers in cells A1 and B1.

Subtraction:

To subtract numbers in Excel, use the **-** operator.

2. **Example:**
    - Type the following formula in a cell: **=A1 - B1**
    - Press "Enter" to get the result of subtracting the number in cell B1 from the number in cell A1.

Multiplication:

For multiplication, use the ***** operator.

3. **Example:**
    - Type the following formula in a cell: **=A1 * B1**
    - Press "Enter" to get the product of the numbers in cells A1 and B1.

Division:

To divide numbers in Excel, use the **/** operator.

4. **Example:**
   - Type the following formula in a cell: **=A1 / B1**
   - Press "Enter" to get the result of dividing the number in cell A1 by the number in cell B1.

Using Cell References:

You can also perform basic arithmetic operations using cell references.

5. **Example:**
   - Assume you have numbers in cells A1 and A2.
   - Type the following formula in a cell: **=A1 + A2**
   - Press "Enter" to get the sum of the numbers in cells A1 and A2.

Using Parentheses:

To control the order of operations, use parentheses.

6. **Example:**
   - Type the following formula in a cell: **=(A1 + B1) * C1**
   - Press "Enter" to get the sum of A1 and B1, then multiply the result by C1.

AutoSum Feature:

7. **AutoSum:**
   - Select a cell below or to the right of a column or row of numbers.
   - Click the "AutoSum" button in the toolbar or press "Alt + =" to automatically create a sum formula.

Absolute and Relative References:

Understanding the concepts of absolute and relative references is essential when copying formulas to other cells. Absolute references, denoted by **$**, remain fixed when copied, while relative references adjust based on their new location.

8. **Example with Absolute Reference:**
   - Type the following formula: **=$A$1 + B1**

- When copied to another cell, the reference to A1 remains fixed.

Error Handling:

Always ensure that your formulas are error-free. Common errors include **#DIV/0!** (division by zero) and **#VALUE!** (incorrect data type).

Understanding and practicing these basic arithmetic operations will lay the foundation for more complex calculations and analyses in Microsoft Excel.

Data Visualization with Charts

Creating Charts in Excel

Creating charts in Microsoft Excel is a powerful way to visually represent and analyze data. Excel provides a variety of chart types, and creating a chart is a straightforward process. Here's a step-by-step guide:

Basic Steps to Create a Chart:

1. **Prepare Your Data:**

    - Organize your data in a worksheet with appropriate column or row headers.

    - Ensure that your data is numerical and well-structured.

2. **Select Data:**

    - Highlight the range of cells you want to include in your chart.

3. **Insert a Chart:**

    - Go to the "Insert" tab in the Excel ribbon.

    - Click on the type of chart you want to create (e.g., "Bar," "Line," "Pie").

Customizing the Chart:

4. **Chart Elements:**

    - Once the chart is inserted, you can customize it by adding or removing elements. Right-click on different parts of the chart to access options.

5. **Chart Styles:**

    - Experiment with different chart styles available in the "Chart Styles" group on the Design tab.

6. **Chart Titles and Labels:**

    - Add or edit chart titles, axis labels, and data labels by clicking on the corresponding elements and typing.

Changing Chart Type:

7. **Change Chart Type:**
   - Right-click on the chart, and select "Change Chart Type" to switch to a different chart style.

Data Series and Axes:

8. **Data Series:**
   - Modify data series by right-clicking on a data point and selecting "Format Data Series." Adjust options like color, fill, and border.

9. **Axes Options:**
   - Right-click on axis labels and choose "Format Axis" to customize axis options.

Advanced Chart Options:

10. **Combination Charts:**
    - Combine different chart types in a single chart for more complex analyses.
    - Select the data series you want to change, right-click, and choose "Chart Type."

11. **Sparklines:**
    - Create small, in-cell charts known as sparklines for a quick visual overview of data trends.
    - Go to the "Insert" tab and select "Line," "Column," or "Win/Loss" under "Sparklines."

Recommended Charts:

12. **Recommended Charts:**
    - Excel offers a "Recommended Charts" feature that suggests suitable chart types based on your data. Select your data, go to the "Insert" tab, and click "Recommended Charts."

Saving and Sharing:

13. **Save and Share:**
    - Save your Excel workbook to retain the chart.
    - You can also copy the chart and paste it into other applications or export it as an image.

Dynamic Charts with Tables:

14. **Create a Table:**
    - Convert your data range into an Excel Table (Insert > Table).
    - When you add new data to the table, the chart will automatically update.

Chart Templates:

15. **Save as Template:**
    - Customize a chart and save it as a template for future use.

Choosing the Right Chart Type

Choosing the right chart type is crucial for effectively visualizing your data and conveying insights. The best chart type depends on the nature of your data and the message you want to communicate. Here are some common types of charts and guidance on when to use them:

1. Column Chart:
- **Use for:** Comparing individual values or showing trends over a discrete set of categories.
- **Example:** Comparing sales figures for different products.

2. Bar Chart:

- **Use for:** Comparing individual values or showing trends over a discrete set of categories (similar to column charts but with horizontal bars).
- **Example:** Comparing the performance of different teams.

3. Line Chart:

- **Use for:** Showing trends over a continuous set of data points or time series.
- **Example:** Plotting stock prices over a period.

4. Pie Chart:

- **Use for:** Showing the proportion of parts to a whole.
- **Example:** Displaying the market share of different products.

5. Area Chart:

- **Use for:** Showing trends over time and emphasizing the magnitude of change.
- **Example:** Displaying the growth of sales over quarters.

6. Scatter Plot:

- **Use for:** Showing the relationship between two variables.
- **Example:** Plotting the correlation between advertising spending and sales.

7. Bubble Chart:

- **Use for:** Displaying three-dimensional data with two variables represented on the axes and the third variable represented by the size of the bubbles.
- **Example:** Showing the relationship between revenue, profit, and market share for different products.

8. Radar Chart:

- **Use for:** Displaying multivariate data in the form of a two-dimensional chart with three or more quantitative variables represented on axes.

- **Example:** Comparing the performance of different athletes in various sports.

9. Histogram:

- **Use for:** Displaying the distribution of a single variable.
- **Example:** Showing the distribution of ages in a population.

10. Combo Chart:

Use for combining different types of charts in a single visualization for a more comprehensive representation of data.

Example: Combining a line chart and a column chart to show both trends and individual values.

Considerations:

- **Data Structure:** The structure of your data (categorical or numerical) influences the choice of chart type.
- **Message Clarity:** Consider the message you want to convey and choose a chart that makes that message clear.
- **Audience:** Tailor your chart choice to your audience's familiarity with different chart types.
- **Avoid Misleading Charts:** Ensure that your choice of chart accurately represents your data and avoids common pitfalls.

Formatting and Customizing Charts
Formatting and Customizing Charts:

1. **Select the Chart:**
    - Click on the chart to select it. Handles and sizing dots will appear around the edges.
2. **Chart Tools:**

- Go to the "Chart Tools" section on the ribbon. Here, you'll find "Design," "Layout," and "Format" tabs specific to chart customization.

Using the Design Tab:

3. **Quick Layouts:**
   - In the "Design" tab, explore the "Chart Layouts" to quickly change the overall look of your chart with different combinations of elements.

4. **Chart Styles:**
   - Choose different predefined styles in the "Chart Styles" group to change the color scheme and appearance of your chart.

Using the Layout Tab:

5. **Axes and Labels:**
   - Use the "Axes" group to add or remove axis titles, change axis scale, or format labels.

6. **Chart Title:**
   - Click on "Chart Title" to add or edit the title of your chart.

7. **Legend:**
   - Customize the legend position or turn it on/off using options in the "Legend" group.

Using the Format Tab:

8. **Format Selection:**
   - Click on individual chart elements (bars, lines, data points) to format them individually.
   - Use the "Format Selection" group to change fill color, border style, effects, etc.

9. **Shape Styles:**

- Apply shape styles to specific chart elements in the "Shape Styles" group.

10. **Chart Elements:**

    - Use the "Chart Elements" dropdown to toggle on/off various chart elements like data labels, trendlines, error bars, etc.

Specific Chart Customization:

11. **Series Options:**

    - Right-click on a data series and choose "Format Data Series" to customize specific data series in the chart.

12. **Axis Options:**

    - Right-click on the axis (X or Y) and choose "Format Axis" to adjust specific axis settings.

Save Chart Template:

13. **Save as Template:**

    - If you have a customized chart style, you can save it as a template for future use.
    - Go to the "Design" tab, click "Save as Template," and provide a name for your custom chart template.

Preview and Finalize:

14. **Preview and Adjust:**

    - Continuously preview your changes by selecting the chart and applying different formatting options until you achieve the desired look.

15. **Save Changes:**

    - Save your Excel workbook to retain the customized chart settings.

Sorting and Filtering Data

Sorting Data in Excel

Sorting data in Microsoft Excel is a common task that allows you to organize information in a specific order. Here's a step-by-step guide on how to sort data:

Sorting a Range of Data:

1. **Select the Range:**
   - Click and drag to select the range of cells you want to sort. Ensure that your selection includes the entire dataset, including headers if applicable.

2. **Go to the "Data" Tab:**
   - Navigate to the "Data" tab on the Excel ribbon.

3. **Sort Ascending (A-Z) or Descending (Z-A):**
   - In the "Sort & Filter" group, click on the "Sort A to Z" (ascending) or "Sort Z to A" (descending) button.
   - Alternatively, you can click the "Sort" button to open the Sort dialog box for more options.

Sorting Options in the Sort Dialog Box:

4. **Sort Dialog Box:**
   - Click the "Sort" button to open the Sort dialog box.

5. **Choose Column to Sort:**
   - In the "Sort by" dropdown, select the column by which you want to sort the data.

6. **Sort Order:**
   - Choose the sort order (ascending or descending) in the "Order" dropdown.

7. **Add Levels:**

- If your data has multiple levels (e.g., sorting first by one column and then by another), you can add additional levels.

8. **Options:**
    - Check the "My data has headers" box if your selected range includes headers.

9. **Sort and Apply:**
    - Click "OK" to apply the sorting.

Sorting by Custom Order:

10. **Custom Sort:**
    - In the Sort dialog box, you can choose "Custom List" to sort based on a custom order.
    - Click "OK" to apply the custom sort order.

Sorting an Excel Table:

11. **Sorting Table Columns:**
    - If your data is organized as an Excel Table, you can click the dropdown arrow in the column header and choose "Sort A to Z" or "Sort Z to A."

Sorting with Keyboard Shortcuts:

12. **Quick Sort:**
    - For a quick sort, select a cell within the column you want to sort and use the keyboard shortcuts:
        - Ascending: **Alt + H + S + A**
        - Descending: **Alt + H + S + D**

Sorting Multiple Columns:

13. **Sorting Multiple Columns:**
    - To sort by multiple columns, select the entire range, open the Sort dialog box, and specify the primary and secondary sorting columns.

14. **Sort Options:**
    - You can choose to sort columns independently or continue with the same sorting order.

Undoing a Sort:

15. **Undoing a Sort:**
    - If you want to undo a sort, press **Ctrl + Z** immediately after the sort operation.

Filtering Data

Filtering data based on specific criteria in Microsoft Excel allows you to focus on and analyze specific portions of your dataset. Here's a step-by-step guide on how to filter data:

Basic Filtering:

1. **Select the Range:**
   - Click and drag to select the range of cells you want to filter. Ensure that your selection includes the entire dataset, including headers if applicable.

2. **Go to the "Data" Tab:**
   - Navigate to the "Data" tab on the Excel ribbon.

3. **Filter:**
   - In the "Sort & Filter" group, click on the "Filter" button. This will add filter arrows to the header row of your selected range.

Applying Filters:

4. **Filter Arrow:**
   - Click on the filter arrow in the header of the column by which you want to filter.

5. **Filter Options:**
   - Choose filter options such as sorting in ascending or descending order, or select specific values to filter.

Multiple Criteria Filtering:

6. **Text Filters:**

    - For text columns, you can use text filters like "Contains," "Begins with," or "Ends with."

7. **Number Filters:**

    - For number columns, you can use number filters like "Equals," "Greater Than," "Less Than," etc.

8. **Date Filters:**

    - For date columns, you can use date filters like "Before," "After," or specific date ranges.

Clearing Filters:

9. **Clear Filter:**

    - To clear a filter and display all data, click the filter arrow and choose "Clear Filter."

Advanced Filter Options:

10. **Filter by Color/Icon:**

    - If you've applied conditional formatting, you can filter by color or icon.

11. **Filter by Selection:**

    - If you want to filter based on a specific cell's value, select that cell, right-click, and choose "Filter" > "Equals Selected Cell's Value."

Multiple Criteria Filtering:

12. **Multiple Criteria:**

    - You can apply filters to multiple columns simultaneously, creating complex criteria.

13. **Custom Filters:**

    - Use the "Custom Filter" option to create more advanced filtering criteria.

Filtered Data Analysis:

14. Analyze Filtered Data:

- Once you've applied filters, you can analyze the filtered data, perform calculations, or create charts based on the visible data.

Clearing Filters:

15. Clear All Filters:

- To clear all filters in the selected range, click the "Clear" button in the "Sort & Filter" group.

Removing Filters:

16. Remove Filters:

- To remove filters entirely, go back to the "Data" tab and click the "Filter" button to toggle off filtering.

Data Protection and Security

Protecting Worksheets and Workbooks

Using Passwords and Permissions

Using passwords and permissions in Microsoft Excel adds an extra layer of security to your workbooks, preventing unauthorized access and controlling what users can do with the data. Here's a guide on how to use passwords and set permissions:

Protecting a Worksheet with a Password:

1. **Select the Worksheet:**
    - Click on the worksheet tab that you want to protect.

2. **Go to the "Review" Tab:**
    - Navigate to the "Review" tab on the Excel ribbon.

3. **Protect Sheet:**
    - In the "Changes" group, click on "Protect Sheet."

4. **Set Password:**
    - Enter a password in the "Password to unprotect sheet" field.

5. **Select Protection Options:**
    - Choose the specific elements you want to protect, such as formatting, inserting/deleting columns or rows, sorting, and filtering.

6. **Click "OK":**
    - Click "OK" to apply the protection.

7. **Enter Password (If Applied):**
    - If you set a password, you will need to enter it to confirm the protection.

Protecting a Workbook with a Password:

8. **Go to the "File" Tab:**

- If you want to protect the entire workbook, go to the "File" tab on the Excel ribbon.

9. **Info and Protect Workbook:**
   - Click on "Info" and then select "Protect Workbook."

10. **Encrypt with Password:**
    - Choose "Encrypt with Password" to set a password for the entire workbook.

11. **Enter Password:**
    - Enter a password and click "OK."

12. **Re-enter Password:**
    - Re-enter the password to confirm.

13. **Save the Workbook:**
    - Save the workbook to apply the protection.

Setting Permissions for Workbook Sharing:

14. **Go to the "Review" Tab:**
    - Navigate to the "Review" tab on the Excel ribbon.

15. **Protect Workbook:**
    - Click on "Protect Workbook" and choose "Protect Structure and Windows."

16. **Set Password (Optional):**
    - Enter a password if you want to secure the structure of the workbook.

17. **Permissions Options:**
    - Choose specific permissions, such as allowing users to insert/delete rows or columns, format cells, or edit objects.

18. **Click "OK":**

- Click "OK" to apply the protection.

19. **Enter Password (If Applied):**

    - If you set a password, you will need to enter it to confirm the protection.

Removing Passwords and Permissions:

20. **Unprotect Worksheet or Workbook:**

    - To remove protection from a worksheet or workbook, go back to the respective "Protect" option in the "Review" tab, enter the password if applicable, and choose "Unprotect."

21. **Clear Password:**

    - If you set a password for a worksheet or workbook, you can clear it by selecting "Unprotect Sheet" or "Unprotect Workbook" and entering the existing password.

Introduction to PivotTables

Creating PivotTables

Creating PivotTables in Microsoft Excel allows you to analyze and summarize large datasets by organizing them into a more manageable format. Here's a step-by-step guide on how to create PivotTables:

Basic PivotTable Creation:

1. **Select Your Data:**
   - Click and drag to select the range of cells containing your data.

2. **Go to the "Insert" Tab:**
   - Navigate to the "Insert" tab on the Excel ribbon.

3. **Click "PivotTable":**
   - In the "Tables" group, click on "PivotTable."

4. **Confirm Data Range:**
   - Make sure the "Create PivotTable" dialog box has the correct data range selected.

5. **Choose Where to Place the PivotTable:**
   - Choose whether you want the PivotTable in a new worksheet or an existing worksheet.

6. **Click "OK":**
   - Click "OK" to create the PivotTable.

PivotTable Field List:

7. **PivotTable Field List:**
   - A new worksheet will appear, and the PivotTable Field List pane will open on the right.

Arranging Fields:

8. **Drag Fields to Rows and Columns:**

- Drag the fields from the PivotTable Field List to the Rows and Columns areas to organize your data.

Adding Values:

9. **Drag Fields to Values:**
   - Drag fields to the Values area to calculate values based on those fields.

Grouping Data:

10. **Group Data (Optional):**
    - You can group data by right-clicking on a date field (for example) and choosing "Group" to create meaningful date groups.

Customizing PivotTable:

11. **Explore PivotTable Tools:**
    - Explore the "PivotTable Tools" in the ribbon for additional options, such as sorting, filtering, and formatting.

Refreshing Data:

12. **Refresh Data:**
    - If your source data changes, right-click on the PivotTable and choose "Refresh" to update the PivotTable.

Creating PivotCharts:

13. **Create PivotChart (Optional):**
    - You can create a PivotChart alongside your PivotTable to visualize the data.

Advanced PivotTable Options:

14. **Explore Advanced Options:**
    - Explore advanced PivotTable options, such as calculated fields and items, to perform custom calculations.

15. **Slicer (Optional):**

- If you want to filter data interactively, you can insert a Slicer from the "Insert" tab.

Saving and Sharing:

16. **Save and Share:**
    - Save your workbook to retain the PivotTable configuration and share the workbook with others.

Modifying and Updating PivotTable:

17. **Modify PivotTable:**
    - To modify the PivotTable, go back to the original data source, make changes, and then refresh the PivotTable.

Removing PivotTable:

18. **Remove PivotTable:**
    - To remove a PivotTable, right-click on the table, and choose "Delete" or simply delete the sheet containing the PivotTable.

Data Import and Export

Importing Data into Excel

Importing data into Excel is a common task that allows you to bring external data into your Excel workbook for analysis and manipulation. Here's a step-by-step guide on how to import data into Excel:

Importing Data from a Text File (CSV):

1. **Open Excel:**
   - Launch Microsoft Excel and open a new or existing workbook.

2. **Go to the "Data" Tab:**
   - Navigate to the "Data" tab on the Excel ribbon.

3. **Get Data from Text:**
   - In the "Get Data" group, click on "From Text" if you have a text file, such as a CSV (Comma Separated Values).

4. **Select Text File:**
   - Choose the text file you want to import and click "Import."

5. **Text Import Wizard:**
   - The Text Import Wizard will guide you through the import process. Choose the delimiter (usually Comma for CSV files) and click "Next."

6. **Column Data Format:**
   - Specify the data format for each column and click "Finish" to complete the import.

7. **Load Data into Excel:**
   - Choose where you want to place the imported data (Table, PivotTable, etc.) and click "OK" to load the data into Excel.

Importing Data from Other Sources:

8. **Go to the "Data" Tab:**
   - Navigate to the "Data" tab on the Excel ribbon.

9. **Get Data from Other Sources:**
    - In the "Get Data" group, click on "Get Data" to import data from other sources like databases, online services, or other file formats.

10. **Choose Data Source:**
    - Select the appropriate data source, such as SQL Server, SharePoint, Web, etc.

11. **Configure Connection:**
    - Configure the connection settings and credentials if required.

12. **Load Data into Excel:**
    - Choose where you want to place the imported data (Table, PivotTable, etc.) and click "OK" to load the data into Excel.

Importing Data from Excel Files:

13. **Go to the "Data" Tab:**
    - Navigate to the "Data" tab on the Excel ribbon.

14. **Get Data from Workbook:**
    - In the "Get Data" group, click on "Get Data" and choose "From Workbook" to import data from another Excel file.

15. **Select Excel File:**
    - Select the Excel file you want to import and click "Import."

16. **Choose Table or Range:**
    - Choose the specific table or range you want to import and click "Load" to bring the data into Excel.

Refreshing Imported Data:

17. **Refresh Data:**
    - If the source data changes, you can right-click on the imported data in Excel and choose "Refresh" to update it.

Exporting Data from Excel

Exporting data from Excel allows you to save your workbook or specific sheets in different file formats, making it easy to share or use the data in other applications. Here's a step-by-step guide on how to export data from Excel:

Save As a Different File Format:

1. **Open Excel:**

    - Launch Microsoft Excel and open the workbook containing the data you want to export.

2. **Go to the "File" Tab:**

    - Navigate to the "File" tab on the Excel ribbon.

3. **Click "Save As":**

    - Click on "Save As" to open the Save As dialog.

4. **Choose Save Location:**

    - Select the folder where you want to save the exported file.

5. **Choose File Format:**

    - In the "Save as type" dropdown, choose the desired file format. Common formats include:

        - Excel Workbook (.xlsx): Standard Excel file format.

        - Excel 97-2003 Workbook (.xls): Compatible with older versions of Excel.

        - CSV (Comma delimited) (.csv): Plain text file with comma-separated values.

        - PDF (.pdf): Portable Document Format.

6. **Enter File Name:**

    - Enter a name for the exported file.

7. **Click "Save":**

- Click "Save" to export the data in the chosen format.

Save a Specific Range as a CSV:

8. **Select Range:**
    - If you want to export a specific range, select the range of cells in your worksheet.

9. **Go to the "File" Tab:**
    - Navigate to the "File" tab on the Excel ribbon.

10. **Click "Save As":**
    - Click on "Save As" to open the Save As dialog.

11. **Choose Save Location:**
    - Select the folder where you want to save the exported file.

12. **Choose File Format - CSV:**
    - In the "Save as type" dropdown, choose "CSV (Comma delimited) (.csv)."

13. **Enter File Name:**
    - Enter a name for the exported CSV file.

14. **Click "Save":**
    - Click "Save" to export the selected range as a CSV file.

Exporting a Chart or Graph:

15. **Select Chart:**
    - If you have a chart or graph in your workbook, select it.

16. **Go to the "File" Tab:**
    - Navigate to the "File" tab on the Excel ribbon.

17. **Click "Save As Picture":**
    - Choose "Save As Picture" to export the selected chart as an image.

18. **Choose Save Location:**
    - Select the folder where you want to save the exported image.

19. **Enter File Name:**
    - Enter a name for the exported image.

20. **Choose Image Format:**
    - Choose the desired image format, such as PNG or JPEG.

21. **Click "Save":**
    - Click "Save" to export the chart as an image.

Save a Worksheet as a PDF:

22. **Select Worksheet:**
    - If you want to export an entire worksheet as a PDF, click on the sheet tab.

23. **Go to the "File" Tab:**
    - Navigate to the "File" tab on the Excel ribbon.

24. **Click "Save As":**
    - Click on "Save As" to open the Save As dialog.

25. **Choose Save Location:**
    - Select the folder where you want to save the exported PDF file.

26. **Choose File Format - PDF:**
    - In the "Save as type" dropdown, choose "PDF (.pdf)."

27. **Enter File Name:**
    - Enter a name for the exported PDF file.

28. **Click "Save":**
    - Click "Save" to export the entire worksheet as a PDF.

Excel Tips and Tricks for Seniors & Beginners

Keyboard Shortcuts for Efficiency

Using keyboard shortcuts can significantly improve your efficiency when working with Excel. Here are some essential keyboard shortcuts for common tasks:

Navigation Shortcuts:

1. **Move to the next cell:**
     - **Windows:** Enter
     - **Mac:** Return

2. **Move to the previous cell:**
     - **Windows:** Shift + Enter
     - **Mac:** Shift + Return

3. **Move one cell to the right:**
     - **Windows/Mac:** Tab

4. **Move one cell to the left:**
     - **Windows/Mac:** Shift + Tab

5. **Move one cell up:**
     - **Windows/Mac:** Up Arrow

6. **Move one cell down:**
     - **Windows/Mac:** Down Arrow

7. **Move to the beginning of the row:**
     - **Windows/Mac:** Home

8. **Move to the beginning of the column:**

- **Windows/Mac:** Ctrl + Up Arrow (Windows), Command + Up Arrow (Mac)

Selection Shortcuts:

9. **Select the entire row:**
   - **Windows/Mac:** Shift + Space

10. **Select the entire column:**
    - **Windows/Mac:** Ctrl + Space (Windows), Command + Space (Mac)

11. **Select the entire worksheet:**
    - **Windows/Mac:** Ctrl + A (Windows), Command + A (Mac)

Editing Shortcuts:

12. **Undo:**
    - **Windows/Mac:** Ctrl + Z (Windows), Command + Z (Mac)

13. **Redo:**
    - **Windows/Mac:** Ctrl + Y (Windows), Command + Y (Mac)

14. **Cut:**
    - **Windows/Mac:** Ctrl + X (Windows), Command + X (Mac)

15. **Copy:**
    - **Windows/Mac:** Ctrl + C (Windows), Command + C (Mac)

16. **Paste:**
    - **Windows/Mac:** Ctrl + V (Windows), Command + V (Mac)

17. **Fill Down:**
    - **Windows/Mac:** Ctrl + D (Windows), Command + D (Mac)

18. **Fill Right:**
    - **Windows/Mac:** Ctrl + R (Windows), Command + R (Mac)

19. **Insert new row:**

- **Windows/Mac:** Ctrl + Shift + "+"

20. **Insert new column:**

    - **Windows/Mac:** Ctrl + Shift + "+"

21. **Delete row:**

    - **Windows/Mac:** Ctrl + "-"

22. **Delete column:**

    - **Windows/Mac:** Ctrl + "-"

Formatting Shortcuts:

23. **Bold:**

    - **Windows/Mac:** Ctrl + B (Windows), Command + B (Mac)

24. **Italic:**

    - **Windows/Mac:** Ctrl + I (Windows), Command + I (Mac)

25. **Underline:**

    - **Windows/Mac:** Ctrl + U (Windows), Command + U (Mac)

26. **Open Format Cells dialog:**

    - **Windows:** Ctrl + 1
    - **Mac:** Command + 1

Workbook Navigation Shortcuts:

27. **Move to the next sheet:**

    - **Windows/Mac:** Ctrl + Page Down (Windows), Command + Page Down (Mac)

28. **Move to the previous sheet:**

    - **Windows/Mac:** Ctrl + Page Up (Windows), Command + Page Up (Mac)

29. **Create a new worksheet:**

- **Windows/Mac:** Shift + F11

30. **Switch to formula view:**

    - **Windows/Mac:** Ctrl + ` (grave accent)

Useful Excel Functions for Beginners

Excel offers a range of powerful functions that can be incredibly useful for beginners. Here are some fundamental Excel functions to get started:

Arithmetic Functions:

1. **SUM:**
    - Adds up a range of numbers.
    - Example: =SUM(A1:A10)

2. **AVERAGE:**
    - Calculates the average of a range of numbers.
    - Example: =AVERAGE(A1:A10)

3. **MAX and MIN:**
    - Finds the maximum or minimum value in a range.
    - Example: =MAX(A1:A10) or =MIN(A1:A10)

Text Functions:

4. **CONCATENATE:**
    - Joins multiple text strings into one.
    - Example: =CONCATENATE(A1," ",B1)

5. **LEN:**
    - Counts the number of characters in a cell.
    - Example: =LEN(A1)

6. **LEFT and RIGHT:**

- Extracts a specified number of characters from the left or right side of a text string.
- Example: =LEFT(A1,5) or =RIGHT(A1,5)

7. **TRIM:**
   - Removes extra spaces from a text string.
   - Example: =TRIM(A1)

Logical Functions:

8. **IF:**
   - Checks a condition and returns one value if the condition is true and another value if false.
   - Example: =IF(A1>10,"Yes","No")

9. **AND, OR:**
   - Checks multiple conditions and returns true or false based on logical tests.
   - Example: =AND(A1>10,B1="Yes") or =OR(A1=10,B1="No")

Date and Time Functions:

10. **TODAY:**
    - Returns the current date.
    - Example: =TODAY()

11. **DATE and DATEVALUE:**
    - Creates a date from year, month, and day values.
    - Example: =DATE(2023,12,31) or =DATEVALUE("12/31/2023")

12. **YEAR, MONTH, DAY:**
    - Extracts the year, month, or day from a date.
    - Example: =YEAR(A1) or =MONTH(A1) or =DAY(A1)

Statistical Functions:

13. COUNT and COUNTA:
- Counts the number of cells that contain numbers or any type of data.
- Example: =COUNT(A1:A10) or =COUNTA(A1:A10)

14. STDEV and STDEVP:
- Calculates the standard deviation of a sample or population.
- Example: =STDEV(A1:A10) or =STDEVP(A1:A10)

15. RAND:
- Generates a random number between 0 and 1.
- Example: `=RAND()`

Common Errors and Troubleshooting
Identifying and Fixing Errors

Identifying and fixing errors in Excel is crucial to ensuring accurate data analysis. Here's a guide on common error types, how to identify them, and ways to resolve them:

Common Types of Errors:
1. **#DIV/0!:** Occurs when attempting to divide by zero.
2. **#VALUE!:** Arises when using the wrong data type or incorrect arguments in a formula.
3. **#REF!:** Indicates a reference error due to an invalid cell reference.
4. **#NAME?:** Occurs when Excel doesn't recognize text within a formula.
5. **#N/A!:** Denotes "Not Available" and appears when a value is missing.

Identifying Errors:
1. **Error Markers:** Cells with errors display a small triangle in the top left corner.
2. **Error Values:** The cell shows the error value instead of the expected result.
3. **Formula Auditing Tools:** Use the "Error Checking" and "Trace Error" options in the "Formulas" tab to identify errors.

Resolving Errors:
1. **#DIV/0!:** Check for zero denominators before division. Use an IF statement to avoid division by zero.
   - Example: **=IF(B1=0,0,A1/B1)**
2. **#VALUE!:** Double-check data types and formatting within formulas. Ensure compatibility among functions used.
   - Example: Verify that text functions receive text data, numeric functions receive numbers, etc.

3. **#REF!:** Review and correct invalid cell references. Check for deleted or moved cells/worksheets used in formulas.

    - Example: Manually correct cell references in formulas.

4. **#NAME?:** Ensure correct function names and syntax.

    - Example: Correct any misspelled function names or references.

5. **#N/A!:** Use functions like IFERROR or IFNA to handle missing values gracefully.

    - Example: **=IFERROR(VLOOKUP(A1, Range, 2, FALSE), "Not Found")**

Excel Tools for Error Resolution:

1. **Error Checking:** Use the "Error Checking" feature in the "Formulas" tab to detect and navigate through errors in the workbook.

2. **Trace Error:** Trace error precedents or dependents using the "Trace Error" options to identify where an error originates or its impact on other cells.

3. **Evaluate Formula:** Step through formulas using the "Evaluate Formula" tool in the "Formulas" tab to understand the calculation process.

4. **Data Validation:** Use data validation to prevent incorrect data entry, reducing the chance of errors in the first place.

Troubleshooting Common Excel Issues

Troubleshooting common Excel issues can help ensure smooth data management and analysis.

1. Excel Crashes or Freezes:

- **Solution:**
  - Check for software updates and install the latest version.
  - Disable unnecessary add-ins.
  - Verify that your computer meets the system requirements for Excel.
  - Repair or reinstall Microsoft Office.

2. Excel Formulas Not Updating:

- **Solution:**
  - Check if the "Automatic" calculation mode is selected in the Formulas tab.
  - Press **F9** to force a recalculation of all formulas.
  - Ensure that there are no circular references.
  - Check for volatile functions (e.g., **NOW()**, **TODAY()**) that can impact recalculation.

3. Data Not Sorting Correctly:

- **Solution:**
  - Ensure that the data range is correctly selected.
  - Check for hidden rows or columns that may affect sorting.
  - Verify that the data does not contain merged cells.

4. Excel File Won't Open:

- **Solution:**
  - Try opening the file in Safe Mode by holding **Ctrl** while launching Excel.

- Check for file corruption. Open a blank workbook, go to Data tab > Get Data > Combine Queries > Merge.
- Attempt to open the file on a different computer.

5. Excel File is Too Large:

- **Solution:**
  - Remove unnecessary formatting and empty cells.
  - Convert large ranges of data to tables.
  - Consider breaking the workbook into smaller, linked files.
  - Use the "Save As" option and choose a different file format like binary **.xlsb** for reduced size.

6. Print Preview Doesn't Match Actual Print:

- **Solution:**
  - Check the print area and page layout settings.
  - Adjust margins and scaling in the Page Layout tab.
  - Verify that the correct printer and paper size are selected.
  - Use the "Page Break Preview" to adjust page breaks.

7. Cannot Copy-Paste Data:

- **Solution:**
  - Check if the cells are locked (protected sheet).
  - Verify that the clipboard is not full.
  - Use the "Paste Special" option to paste values or formats only.

8. Cell Formatting Issues:

- **Solution:**
  - Use the "Clear" function to remove formatting from cells.
  - Check for conditional formatting rules that might override manual formatting.
  - Verify regional settings for date and number formats.

9. Graphs/Charts Not Displaying Properly:
   - **Solution:**
     - Ensure that the data source for the chart is correct.
     - Check for hidden or filtered data that might affect the chart.
     - Adjust chart settings, titles, and axis labels as needed.

10. Error Messages in Formulas:

Solution: Hover over the error to see a tooltip with details. - Check for correct syntax and proper cell references. - Use the "Evaluate Formula" tool in the Formulas tab to debug.

11. Missing Data after Filtering:

Solution: Ensure that all rows have the same structure. - Verify that the filter range covers all data. - Remove any blank rows within the data range.

Conclusion

Computers for Beginners and seniors" provides a comprehensive and accessible guide aimed at empowering individuals who are new to the digital world or navigating their later years. The book covers a range of essential topics, from understanding computer hardware and software to mastering common applications and troubleshooting issues.

Starting with the basics of computer terminology and functionality, the book progresses to in-depth discussions on operating systems like Windows and macOS. Seniors and beginners are guided through the process of setting up and customizing their computers, ensuring a user-friendly experience.

The chapters on internet security, social media, and multimedia not only equip readers with the necessary skills for online navigation but also emphasize the importance of privacy and safe digital practices. The inclusion of step-by-step guides for popular social media platforms ensures that users can connect with friends and family effortlessly.

The sections on Microsoft Word and Excel offer a hands-on approach to document creation and spreadsheet management, providing a solid foundation for productive computer use. Additionally, the troubleshooting and error resolution guides empower readers to identify and resolve common issues independently.

By focusing on practical applications and incorporating keyboard shortcuts, the book emphasizes efficiency and ease of use, ensuring that seniors and beginners can navigate the digital landscape with confidence. The inclusion of troubleshooting tips and solutions enhances the user experience, making the learning journey smoother and more enjoyable.

Computers for Beginners and seniors is a valuable resource that not only imparts essential computer skills but also fosters a sense of digital literacy and independence. Whether exploring the basics or delving into more advanced features, this guide is tailored to meet the diverse needs of seniors and beginners, enabling them to harness the power of technology for communication, productivity, and personal enrichment.

Printed in Great Britain
by Amazon